American Troublemakers

Thomas Paine: Revolutionary Author

AMERICAN TROUBLEMAKERS

Titles in Series

Cesar Chavez by Burnham Holmes

Jefferson Davis by Robert R. Potter

Mother Jones by Joan C. Hawxhurst

Thomas Paine by Karin Clafford Farley

Sitting Bull by Steven Bodow

Ida B. Wells by Richard M. Haynes

T★★AMERICAN★★S TROUBLEMAKERS

THOMAS PAINE:
Revolutionary Author

Karin Clafford Farley

With an Introduction by James P. Shenton

RSVP
RAINTREE
STECK-VAUGHN
PUBLISHERS
The Steck-Vaughn Company

Austin, Texas

To my daughter, Daryl Lynn Farley

CONSULTANTS

Elizabeth Blackmar
Associate Professor of History
Department of History
Columbia College
New York, New York

Robert M. Goldberg
Consultant to the Social Studies
    Department
(former Department Chair)
Oceanside Middle School
Oceanside, New York

MANAGING EDITOR
Richard G. Gallin

PROJECT MANAGER
Cynthia Ellis

PHOTO EDITOR
Margie Foster

A Gallin House Press Book

Library of Congress Cataloging-in-Publication Data
Farley, Karin Clafford
     Thomas Paine: Revolutionary Author / written by Karin Clafford Farley.
          p.   cm. — (American Troublemakers)
     "A Gallin House Press Book." — T.p. verso
     Includes bibliographical references and index.
     Summary: A biography of the writer and political philosopher whose works influenced the American colonists in their revolt against Great Britian.
     ISBN 0-8114-2329-8
     1. Thomas Paine, 1737-1809 — Juvenile literature.   2. Political scientists — United States — Biography — Juvenile literature.
3. Revolutionaries —United States — Biography — Juvenile literature.
[1. Paine, Thomas, 1737-1809.   2. Political scientists.]   I.Title.   II. Series.
JC178.V2F37   1994
320.5'1'092—dc20
[B]   92-17662
                                                                                                CIP
                                                                                                 AC

Printed and bound in the United States.

1 2 3 4 5 6 7 8 9 0 LB   99 98 97 96 95 94 93

CONTENTS

Map

Thomas Paine

INTRODUCTION

by James P. Shenton

Biography is the history of the individual lives of men and women. In all lives, there is a sequence that begins with birth, evolves into the development of character in childhood and adolescence, is followed by the emergence of maturity in adulthood, and finally concludes with death. All lives follow this pattern, although with each emerge the differences that make each life unique. These distinctive characteristics are usually determined by the particular area in which a person has been most active. An artist draws his or her specific identity from the area of the arts in which he or she has been most active. So the writer becomes an author; the musician, a performer or composer; the politician, a senator, governor, president, or statesperson. The intellectual discipline to which one is attached identifies the scientist, historian, economist, literary critic, or political scientist, among many. Some aspects of human behavior are identified as heroic, cowardly, corrupt, or just ordinary. The task of the biographer is to explain why a particular life is worth remembering. And if the effort is successful, the reader draws from it insights into a vast range of behavior patterns. In a sense, biography provides lessons from life.

Some lives become important because of the position a person holds. Typical would be that of a U.S. President in which a biographer compares the various incumbents to determine their comparative importance. Without question, Abraham Lincoln was a profoundly significant President, much more so than Warren G. Harding whose administration was swamped by corruption. Others achieve importance because of their role in a particular area. So Emily Dickinson and Carl Sandburg are recognized as important poets and Albert Einstein as a great scientist.

Implicit in the choice of biographical subjects is the idea that each somehow affected history. Their lives explain something about the world in which they lived, even as they affect our lives and that of generations to come. But there is another consideration: Some lives are more interesting than those of others. Within each life is a great story that illuminates human behavior.

Then there are those people who are troublemakers, people whom we cannot ignore. They are the people who both upset and fascinate us. Their singular quality is that they are uniquely different. Troublemakers are irritating, perhaps frightening, frustrating, and disturbing, but never dull. They march to their own drummer, and they are original.

Some people are born revolutionaries. Thomas Paine was such a person. Born into an inconspicuous family in England, his youth and early manhood pointed toward an ordinary life as a minor public official. Soon, however, he gained a reputation as a troublemaker. Dismissed from his job and heavily in debt, he decided to go to the British colonies in America. His friend Benjamin Franklin, who was then living in England, assured him that humble origins were not an obstacle to advancement in America. Paine arrived in Philadelphia in late 1774 and quickly involved himself in the revolutionary politics engulfing the 13 colonies.

In his famous 1776 pamphlet *Common Sense*, Paine denounced King George III and the British aristocracy. He urged the people to make a complete break with Britain. On July 4, 1776, the independence that he preached was declared. In the fighting that followed, Paine served well and urged on the rebelling Americans in *The Crisis*, a series of trenchant essays.

A victorious United States returned to peace in 1783. Although he had gained fame, Paine was restless. He crossed the Atlantic to France and found another country in which the old order was coming apart. At first, he supported the French Revolution. His powerfully written *The Rights of Man* bluntly proclaimed the equality of all humanity. In England, Paine was declared an outlaw. In France, he was elected to the National Convention. But by late 1793, Paine was imprisoned. Only by the barest of margins did he escape the guillotine.

Not until 1802 did Paine return to the United States. But his *Age of Reason*, a scathing attack on organized religion, had gained him enemies. His health shattered, the man who helped shape two revolutions went to a lonely grave. In three countries, though, he would be remembered as the revolutionary troublemaker.

CHAPTER ONE

Poor Tom Pain

In mid-18th-century, kings and queens ruled almost all countries. The royal families, the nobles, and the leaders of the church owned most of the land. Below them in wealth and power were high government officials, doctors, and lawyers, and large business owners like bankers and merchants. Next came the small farmers and shopkeepers who were often skilled craftsmen. They made enough money to live very modestly. The majority of the people in rural areas were poor peasants; the cities were crowded with unskilled laborers. These wretchedly poor people often did not have enough good food to eat to stay healthy, a decent roof over their heads to keep out the cold and rain, nor enough clothing to keep them warm.

One of the reasons the poor were kept poor was that they did not own land. Most of the little money they earned went to pay rent to the rich landowners. And they had to pay heavy taxes to support the kings' constant wars with each other. The poor were allowed no voice in how they were treated. In most countries, the kings were all-powerful. Few dared speak out against them. Anyone who did might meet a horrible death for treason. Most people lived this way century after century.

Tom Pain's father Joseph was a stay maker, a skilled craftsman who made parts for women's corsets. Women usually could only afford one corset in their lifetime. A stay maker did not sell a great many stays especially in such a small town as Thetford, England, where Joseph Pain lived. Although he was an independent businessman, a stay maker was at the low end of tradesmen, below a carpenter, silversmith, butcher, or even candlemaker.

The family lived in a small, gray, stone row house on Bridge Street. The house had two rooms upstairs and two down. One of the rooms was the shop and workroom. Joseph Pain was one of

An 18th-century English village. Thomas Pain was born in Thetford in 1737. He added an "e" to his last name 39 years later.

the lucky men in the village who owned a few acres where he raised some food so his family would have enough to eat.

Joseph and his wife Frances's first child was born on January 29, 1737. They named him Thomas. He was to be their only child. A baby daughter born later died in infancy. Most poor boys went to work at the age of seven and gave their tiny wages to help their families. But Tom's parents sent him to the village grammar school when he was six. He learned practical subjects like reading, writing, basic mathematics, and some science. However, Tom's father had him excused from learning Latin. Joseph Pain was a member of the religious Society of Friends, whose members were called Quakers. He did not want his son to learn the ideas of the ancient Romans and Greeks. That was not Christian, Joseph Pain believed. Tom was a bright but rather lazy boy. He did not want to be bothered with the drudgery of learning a dead language like Latin anyway. After all, only churchmen, lawyers, and doctors used Latin.

That Tom did not learn Latin was shortsightedness by a father who gave much love and what little he could afford to his only child. A knowledge of Latin might have given Tom a better chance to rise to a higher station in life and become a lawyer like his Grandfather Cocke. His mother, Frances Cocke, was from one of Thetford's first families.

Tom's favorite subject in school was science. Science fascinated many people in the 1700s. The Age of Enlightenment had started during the previous century. It was strongly influenced by the discoveries of the famous scientist and mathematician Sir Isaac Newton. During the Enlightenment, many educated people began to discard superstitions and beliefs held for centuries.

The experiments of the famous English mathematician and scientist Issac Newton (1642–1727) inspired many people including Pain.

11

They asked how and for what reason things happen. Newton had asked why an apple fell down off a tree, and he discovered gravity. One discovery led to another and then another. Some discoveries were even beginning to make life better for people.

Tom's other education came from the church. Although his father was a Quaker, his mother insisted he be raised in the Church of England. Tom was baptized as an infant and confirmed when he was eight by the bishop of Norwich. He had to learn his catechism—a list of questions and answers about religious beliefs—and memorize long passages from the Bible. But the things he learned puzzled him. He could not understand why God had let his son Jesus die. He wrote later, "I revolted at the recollection of what I had heard, . . . God was too good to do such an action, and also too almighty to be under any necessity of doing it."

Tom's father was 11 years younger than his mother. Tom was closer to his father and loved him dearly. Tom often accompanied him to Quaker meetings. The Quakers did not believe in formal worship services nor were they led by clergymen. They held meetings in very plain buildings called meetinghouses or in members' homes. Anyone was free to stand up and preach or pray when he or she felt like it. This was very different from the ceremonies and cathedrals of the Church of England. Quakers lived simply, wearing plain clothes in a time when people, especially the rich, dressed in lace and velvets. The most outstanding of Quaker beliefs was nonviolence. Most refused to fight in wars, and many strongly opposed slavery.

To attend meetings with his father, Tom had to pass the town gaol (jail), which was next to the Quaker meetinghouse. Outside the jail were a whipping post and the stocks. As punishment for breaking laws, men and women might be tied to the post and publicly whipped. Sometimes criminals' feet and hands were bent and held through holes in large pieces of wood called stocks. Hangings were common because death was the punishment for more than 200 crimes. Even children were executed for minor offenses like shoplifting. Poor people who could not afford clever lawyers were more likely to be punished than rich people. Executed criminals, even children, were hung in chains from the

A Quaker meeting. Pain's father was a member of the Society of Friends, or Quakers, which works for peace.

gibbet, an upright post with a projecting piece of wood, as a warning to others.

Schooling for Tom ended at the age of 13. It was time for him to enter an apprenticeship with a master artisan, or craftsman. The apprentice system was the way boys learned a trade or craft so they could earn a living when they became adults. Parents of the apprentice and the master craftsman signed a legal document in which the master promised to teach his trade to the boy and provide him with food, clothing, and shelter. The apprentice usually lived at his master's house. He had to work hard, keep his master's secrets, and obey his lawful commands. An apprentice was practically a slave for seven years. He was not paid any wages. The skills he learned were considered payment enough. In fact, parents had to pay the master to teach their sons. But Tom Pain's parents could not afford the £40 (about $180) they would have had to pay a master to teach their son. Tom had to be apprenticed to his own father and learn stay making.

Sitting at a bench for long hours six days a week working at stay-making tasks he hated made Tom restless. Like most boys, he dreamed of adventure beyond his village. One of his teachers,

13

the Reverend William Knowles, had once served in the British navy aboard a man-of-war vessel. He had entertained his students with exciting tales of life at sea. Tom had also read a book that made him long to leave Thetford. "I happened, when a school-boy, to pick up a pleasing natural history of Virginia, and my inclination from that day of seeing the western side of the Atlantic never left me." In 1754, war broke out in North America between the British and the French over their colonies. The British called it the French and Indian War because the French formed alliances with American Indian tribes. With the war, Tom saw his chance to get to America. The seaport of Harwich was some 30 miles away—a day's walk for a strong boy. The port was full of privateers whose owners were looking for crews. A privateer was a ship owned by an individual or company. Such a ship was commissioned by its government to arm itself and fight or harass the ships of an enemy country. Usually privateers attacked merchant ships, which were trading vessels used to carry products from port to port. The spoils, the goods that were captured, were then divided among the ship's captain, the owners, the crew, and the king. It was a risky business, but highly profitable if the privateer was not captured—or sunk.

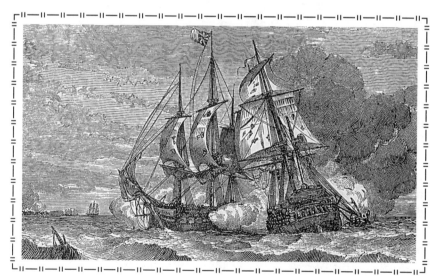

In the 18th-century, ships called privateers were licensed by governments to attack enemy treasure and merchant ships.

Tom ran away from home and headed for Harwich. He later described his adventure this way:

> At an early period, little more than sixteen years of age, raw, adventurous, and heated with the false heroism of a master who had served in a man-of-war, I began the carver of my own fortune, and entered on board the *Terrible* privateer, Captain Death. From this adventure I was happily prevented by the affectionate and moral remonstrance of a good father, who, from his own habits of life, being of Quaker profession, must have begun to look upon me as lost.

What services a stay maker's apprentice could offer a Captain Death probably never occurred to Tom. Certainly his former teacher, the Reverend William Knowles, did not mention that conditions aboard ships at sea were shocking in the 1700s. The food had usually rotted. Dreadful punishments like floggings, keelhaulings, and hangings were meted out to sailors for the slightest infraction of rules. Life was so terrible for sailors that groups called press-gangs roamed the towns kidnapping young men and dragging them aboard ships to serve as crew members. Although Tom had already signed onto the *Terrible*, his father had no great difficulty getting him off. Apprentices belonged to their masters. Tom returned home with his father, but he followed the adventures of the *Terrible*. He wrote later, "The Terrible privateer, Captain Death, stood the hottest engagement of any ship last war."

Two years later, the Seven Years' War broke out in Europe and involved almost all European countries and their colonies. Tom ran away again and this time succeeded in signing aboard another privateer, *The King of Prussia*. Tom did not write about what he did or where he went on *The King of Prussia*. But he must not have liked the life of a sailor because he stayed only about a year. How he managed to escape from a privateer in time of war is not known. He did not return to Thetford, however. Instead, he lost himself in the crowds of London.

15

London in 1757 was the largest city in Europe. Tom was fortunate to find work as a stay maker for a man named Morris who owned a shop on Hanover Street. When he was not working, Tom attended philosophical (science) lectures given by Benjamin Martin and James Ferguson. Martin was a well-known mathematician who wrote books so people not trained in science could understand the subject. Ferguson invented interesting machines and lectured on astronomy. Somehow young Tom Pain also became acquainted with Dr. John Bevis, the foremost astronomer in England, and was allowed to look through Bevis's telescope. That experience of seeing the heavens deeply impressed him. Tom saved part of his meager salary and purchased a pair of globes. He also bought an orrery, a small working model of the solar system.

Attending these lectures and meeting scientists were special occasions. Every day Tom lived as did the poor people of London who were crammed into houses on narrow streets. People did not have modern plumbing. They dumped human waste and garbage into the streets. The result was that the streets were open sewers. Fresh water was so polluted that people dared not drink it for fear of getting sick. Instead, many men, women, and even children drank large amounts of wine and gin. There was much illness and a high death rate.

Tom Pain worked in London only a year. Probably he saw the advantages of small-town living. He moved to Dover on the English Channel and found work with another stay maker—a Mr. Grace. Again Tom remained at that job only a year. In 1759, he moved on to Sandwich. There Tom opened his own shop as a stay maker in a tiny two-story building at 20 New Street.

Tom Pain was 22 years old and free to do as he pleased. Tall for the times, five feet nine inches, and slender with wavy hair, he was considered rather handsome. He had unusual features: a large nose, quite red cheeks, and intensely blue eyes. His eyes were what people noticed first about him.

Certainly the young women noticed him. With his own shop, Tom needed a wife to help him. He met Mary Lambert, an orphan who worked as a maid in the house of a well-to-do wool merchant. In September 1759 at the church of St. Peter in the town of Sandwich, Tom Pain and Mary Lambert were married.

Even with Mary to help him, Tom could not make his business profitable. He became loaded down with debt. At that time, people who did not pay their debts could be thrown into debtors' prison. There they stayed until their family or friends managed to come up with the money to pay the debts. In the middle of a dark night, Tom and Mary Pain sneaked out of Sandwich. They moved to the town of Margate in Kent.

A short time later Mary died. The next year, Tom gave up being a stay maker. He could not earn even the barest living.

Thomas Pain was in his early twenties when he married for the first time. His wife died within a year of the marriage.

CHAPTER TWO

The Tax Collector

Tom Pain decided to try a new occupation. His wife's father had been an officer in Britain's Customs and Excise Service, in other words, a tax collector. It was a humble living, £50 a year, but it was a steady income.

To become an excise officer, Pain would have to pass an examination. But to prepare for the exam required a year or more of study. Pain swallowed his pride, admitted failure, and returned to his parents' home in Thetford. He studied mathematics and the art of writing concise, understandable English. An excise tax collector had to write many reports as part of his work.

After 14 months of study, Pain passed the test, but this did not guarantee him employment. There was a waiting list of many men for any opening. To get an appointment, a person had to know a "great man," someone in a high position. Tom Pain's family did know someone in a high position, Frederick Falkland. He was a member of the Excise Board, which oversaw the work of excise tax collectors. On August 8, 1764, Pain was appointed tax collector to the town of Alford and the surrounding area in Lincolnshire.

No tax collector was liked, but customs and excise tax collectors were especially hated. They collected taxes on liquor, tobacco, tea, and other items small shopkeepers sold. The shopkeepers then had to charge their customers more for these simple pleasures. As a result, smuggling was widespread. The people of the towns considered smugglers their friends and the excisemen their enemies. Part of Pain's work was to catch smugglers. He patrolled on horseback a deserted stretch of beach along the North Sea. It was a dangerous job. Excisemen were sometimes killed in their encounters with smugglers.

Not only was the pay of excise tax collectors fairly low, but they were overloaded with work. They sometimes took a shopkeeper's word about the amount of taxable goods in his store. Without actually inspecting it, they stamped the shopkeeper's account pages as accurate. Pain was caught by his superiors "stamping" accounts in July 1765. He admitted he was guilty of the charges. But his honesty did not undo his laziness in the eyes of the Excise Board. He was dismissed on August 29, 1765.

Within a few months, he found work again as a stay maker in the town of Diss near Thetford. The job in Diss lasted only a short time. He moved on to London where he had no friends or family. When he could not find steady work, he became homeless, living in the streets.

Within ten months after his dismissal, he was desperate. He wrote a letter to the Excise Board begging to be reinstated. His friend Frederick Falkland came to his aid once more. Pain was reinstated the day after his letter was received. But again there were no openings; his name had to go on another waiting list.

Meanwhile, Pain found a position as a teacher of English in a school run by a Mr. Noble. For this position, he was paid only £25 a year—half what he earned as an excise tax collector. In January he obtained a better position teaching in a school in the Kensington section of London run by a Mr. Gardiner. Pain scratched out a living this way for over a year. In May 1767, he had been offered a position as a tax collector in Cornwall. But because of smugglers Cornwall was known to be so dangerous an area that he refused it. Not until February 1768 was he appointed tax collector at the village of Lewes.

Lewes was a town of 5,000 people south of London. Tom Pain liked it immediately. He wanted the town to like him, too. He began referring to himself as "an officer of revenue," instead of the unpopular term *excise officer.*

Pain rented a room at Bull House on High Street. It belonged to Samuel Ollive, who ran a tobacco shop. Ollive was also one of the two constables who carried out the directions of the town council. He liked Pain and introduced him to the leading citizens of Lewes. Pain made friends, for he was a genial man when he wanted to be. Before long, he was attending town meetings and had become a member of the vestry, or governing board, of St. Michael's Church.

Bull House in the town of Lewes. Pain rented a room there and eventually married the landlord's daughter.

Pain became so admired that he was appointed to the Society of Twelve, which served as the town council. The society could levy and collect taxes, issue bonds, and make town improvements on water and road conditions. This service gave Pain practical experience in government at the local level.

During the day, Pain could be seen going about the town with his measuring stick and a bottle of ink. He took his duties as a tax collector very seriously, trying to be fair to the small merchants yet collect the taxes lawfully due the government. Tom Pain never squeezed the shopkeepers for bribes to get more income for himself. His evenings were spent at the White Hart Tavern, the social center of Lewes. He could tell such witty stories that he was soon included in the Headstrong Club, a society that met there. This fun-loving group bestowed the nickname "Commodore" on Pain. He fancied himself an expert on naval affairs after his year at sea aboard *The King of Prussia.*

Pain's friends liked to hear him recite poetry he had written. He had been writing rhymes since he was in the grammar school in Thetford. His parents had discouraged him, but he continued writing his poems secretly.

He dared to read them a poem he had written about the young English general James Wolfe and the French general Louis Montcalm. Both died heroes in the Battle of Quebec in 1759 during the French and Indian War. The Headstrong Club put the poem to music and sang it with much gusto. The fame of this song spread locally. A Mr. Rumbald was so impressed that he paid Pain three guineas (3 pounds, 3 shillings) to write a campaign song to help him win election to Parliament. This was more than what Thomas Pain earned in three whole weeks as a tax collector.

But what Pain enjoyed most were the debates among his new friends of the Headstrong Club. He loved talk, and he liked brandy. The more brandy he drank, the better he talked. He bragged that he seldom read books, but he pored over newspapers every day. Instead of greeting people he met with a "good day," Pain always asked, "What news?" Pain could also argue strongly for his ideas and usually won the debates. His friends awarded him the title "General of the Headstrong War."

Tom Pain was happily settled in his new life when Samuel Ollive, the constable and tobacco shop owner from whom he rented a room, died in July 1769. Mrs. Ollive and her daughter Elizabeth had no experience operating a business. The three Ollive sons were still children. Pain offered to help them in his spare time. He did the bookkeeping and shredded the large tobacco leaves into suitable quantities to sell. The Ollive women needed Pain in the family, and Pain needed a permanent roof over his head and more income. It was decided that he should marry Elizabeth Ollive. Tom was 34 and Elizabeth 13 years younger than he. They were wed in St. Michael's Church across from Bull House on March 26, 1771. Although Elizabeth was young and pretty, this marriage was a business arrangement, not a love match. For when a woman married in the 1700s, all her property went to her husband. Pain later wrote an essay on unhappy marriages part of which described his own. "There are persons in the world who are young without passions, and in health without appetite: these hunt out a wife as they go to *Smithfield* for a horse; and intermarry fortunes, not minds, or even bodies."

The marriage certificate of Thomas Pain and Elizabeth Ollive. Pain continued his work as a tax collector and shopkeeper.

Once in the family, Pain decided to expand the business. He stocked the shop with food, some china, and liquors to attract more customers and increase profits. Pain hoped to profit as an excise officer, too. He was becoming known as an outstanding tax collector. Letters of praise for his reports were sent to him from the Excise Board members in London. He had visions of being promoted.

Early in 1772, excise officers from all over England decided to apply to Parliament for a raise in salary. Their annual pay of £50 a year had remained the same for 100 years, while the cost of living had risen over 25 percent in the previous four years. Having heard of Pain, a group of them asked him to present their case to Parliament. Pain was reluctant to take on this task, although he certainly was in favor of the plan. To manage this work, Pain

The Houses of Parliament. Pain distributed his pamphlet in favor of a pay raise for excise tax collectors to members of Parliament.

knew he had to leave Lewes and go to London where Parliament met. This would cost money. But his friend Frederick Falkland and another member of the Excise Board, George Lewis Scott, urged him to represent the excise tax collectors.

Pain wrote up a petition for the increase in salary and sent it to all the excise officers throughout England to sign. When they returned it, they were asked to enclose three shillings to cover Pain's expenses in London. This brought in about £500. Pain wrote a paper explaining the problems of the excise tax collectors

23

and why they needed a raise. He had 4,000 copies printed up in pamphlet form entitled *The Case of the Officers of Excise.* Pain personally distributed 3,000 to members of Parliament and other influential officials. The rest he sent to the excise officers around England.

Pain was very specific in explaining the problem in pounds, shillings, and pence. He figured the excise men earned much less than £50 in take-home pay: "After tax, charity and sitting expenses are deducted there remains very little more than forty-six pounds; and the expenses of horsekeeping in many places cannot be brought under fourteen pounds a year, besides the purchase at first, and the hazard of life." He estimated they earned "thirty-two pounds per annum, or one shilling and ninepence farthing per day." (This amounted to less than what a skilled craftman earned, or about what an unskilled messenger or porter earned a year.) Yet they collected £4,600,000 per year, the second highest source of revenue to the British Treasury.

Pain went on to restate in many ways how this poverty affected people and the government. "Poverty, in defiance of principle, begets a degree of meanness that will stoop to almost anything. . . . An augmentation of salary sufficient to enable them to live honestly and competently would produce more good effect than all the laws of the land can enforce."

Of course, the cause was lost before it began. Parliament feared other public employees might start asking for raises, too. They could not allow that to happen. England's treasury was empty after the French and Indian War and the Seven Years' War. Pain well understood how Parliament worked because his father was one of only 31 men out of 2,000 people in Thetford who could vote for representatives in Parliament. One house of Parliament, the House of Commons, was made up of representatives from all parts of Britain supposedly elected by the people of towns and districts called boroughs to make laws. But the 31 men of Thetford were told how to vote by the Duke of Grafton, who owned most of the land in and around town. Grafton was also a member of the other house of Parliament, the House of Lords. With only 31 men allowed to vote but told whom to vote for, the 2,000 people of Thetford did not have a voice in government.

Their problems were ignored. Thetford politics was typical of villages all over Britain. It was eventually called the pocket borough system. Parliament did not represent the majority of the British people. It responded only to the needs of the king and other rich and powerful men of Britain.

Tom Pain stayed in London speaking to members of Parliament, the Excise Board, and any other person whose ear he could catch. He refused to admit his cause was doomed. Often, he was in the company of George Lewis Scott. Scott was an expert mathematician and scientist as well as a member of the Excise Board. He had been a tutor to King George III during his childhood and told Pain many stories about the young prince and the court. As a scientist, he also was well acquainted with Ferguson, Martin, and Bevis. Through Scott, Pain renewed his acquaintance with these famous scientists.

Another man of science Pain was introduced to during this stay in London was the American Benjamin Franklin. His experiments with electricity had won him a membership in the Royal Society of London for the Promotion of Natural Knowledge, the oldest scientific society in the world. Franklin had been in London for 18 years as an agent from the colonies in their tax disputes with Parliament. He could easily understand the great difficulties of Pain's campaign with Parliament. Franklin had been through a number of parliamentary wars himself.

Franklin with a member of the House of Lords.

When the excisemen's petitions were officially rejected by Parliament, Pain had no choice but to return to Lewes. During the almost two years he had been in London, the tobacco and grocery shop had failed and was in debt. That was not the end of his troubles. The enemies he made in London outnumbered his friends. He was officially notified on April 8, 1774, that he had again been discharged from the Excise

GEORGE III

Pain criticized the huge salary of King George III.

Service. The reason given for his dismissal was that he had been absent without obtaining the board's permission. Also mentioned was the fact he had been discharged once before. These official reasons covered up the unofficial reason—Pain was considered a troublemaker.

He was angry about what he considered unfair treatment of a loyal worker. Thomas Pain believed he was doing what the whole Excise Service wanted, and he had worked hard. He blamed King George III personally. During the same period, the king had been given a raise of £100,000 for a total salary of £1 million a year by Parliament. Thomas Pain later wrote about this, and his deep feelings of anger can be seen in his words. "It is inhuman to talk of a million sterling a year, paid out of the public taxes of any country, for the support of an individual, whilst thousands who are forced to contribute thereto, are pining with want, and struggling with misery."

Without a salary, he could not pay off the debts of the shop. On April 15 and 16, 1774, his horse and the contents and tools of the shop were sold at public auction to satisfy people to whom he and the Ollives owed money.

There no longer remained any reason for Tom and Elizabeth to continue their marriage. They agreed on a legal separation. As part of the separation agreement, Pain gave up his right to any money or property she owned before their marriage or might acquire in the future. Because she was legally separated from her husband, she could carry on any trade or business as if she were a single woman, a *feme sole*—a married woman who was independent of her husband. Why they did not get a divorce or an annulment leaving them both free to remarry is not known. Most likely this was because of the extreme difficulty of getting a divorce in 18th-century England. Divorce required an act of Parliament and approval by the Church of England. They never saw or even wrote to each other again. Pain later wrote about his marriage, "Thus, as their [a couple's] expectations of pleasure are not very great, neither is the disappointment very grievous."

Pain was sympathetic to the plight of women all over the world. In his writings, he recognized they were very put upon by men and by society. But he did not worry about, provide for, or even grieve for his own wives.

With no wife, no home, and no job, Pain felt he had to leave Lewes. For what, he did not know. He faced the fact that he did not understand business. But he had always known the "natural bent of my mind was to science." He headed for London and got in touch with his scientific friends again. In meetings with Benjamin Franklin, he talked about his need to start over at the age of 37. Franklin encouraged Pain to try his luck in America. After all, Franklin himself was born the 15th of 17 children to a poor candlemaker in Boston. He had risen to a position of wealth and great respect. Franklin was living proof a man could work his way up in America from the humble beginnings both he and Pain shared. Pain had a hard time really believing Franklin. Such a rise in class was rarely possible in England. On Pain's behalf, Franklin dashed off letters of introduction to his son-in-law Richard Bache, who was a merchant in Philadelphia, and to his son, William, who was the royal governor of New Jersey.

Pain was more than ready to leave England. He booked first-class passage on the *London Packet* in October 1774 and set sail for Philadelphia. Although he thought he had chosen his ship carefully, everyone came down with "putrid fever" as Pain called it. When five died, Pain was sure he would never live to see America. The journey took nine weeks. By the time the ship docked in Philadelphia on November 30, 1774, Pain was too ill to leave his bunk, let alone the ship.

CHAPTER THREE

The New World

When the *London Packet* with its stricken passengers tied up at a wharf along Front Street, in Philadelphia, no one was allowed to disembark. Dr. John Kearsley was sent for in order to check the travelers first. He found Thomas Pain so ill that he could not even turn over in his bunk. When the doctor learned that Pain carried letters from Benjamin Franklin, he immediately called for two of his men to bring a stretcher and a carriage. Dr. Kearsley had Pain carried to his own house where he cared for him. Pain probably would not have survived so serious an illness otherwise. As it was, his recovery took over six weeks.

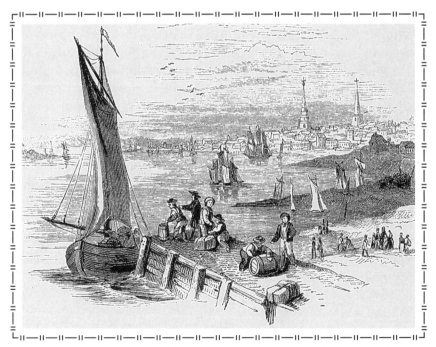

A view of Philadelphia's harbor in the 1770s. The city was the largest in Great Britain's North American colonies.

As his health improved, Pain began reading newspapers again. He learned that he had landed in the middle of a fight, and the center of it was in Philadelphia. Pain wrote that "the country, into which I had just put my foot, was set on fire about my ears."

The treaty ending the French and Indian War in 1763 had given the British all of Canada and whatever land they had not before controlled from the Atlantic Ocean to the Mississippi River except for Florida and New Orleans, which Spain controlled. The British had to protect this vast land they had won from attacks by the French, the Spanish, and some of the American Indian tribes. The British government stationed an army of 10,000 men in North America. It cost the British Treasury £300,000 (over $1 million) a year. Parliament decided to tax the colonists to help pay for the army. After all, the soldiers were protecting them.

In 1764, Parliament put a tax on molasses, coffee, and sugar. It was called the Sugar Act. In 1765, Parliament passed another law, called the Stamp Act. Special stamps had to be bought and stuck onto deeds, mortgages, diplomas, even playing cards and newspapers. The stamp tax angered the colonists even more than the sugar tax did. They proclaimed that "taxation without representation is tyranny." They held protest meetings and marches. In many of the colonies people demanded an end to the Stamp Act. A mob in Boston destroyed the stamp office, made an effigy, or dummy, of the tax collector, and then burned it. Delegates from several colonies met at a Stamp Act Congress to protest. In 1766, Parliament finally repealed the Stamp Act.

But Parliament had also passed a Quartering Act in 1765. Colonists were required to provide British soldiers with fuel, candles, and spirits and housing in barracks or in empty buildings or inns. The colonists were furious. But Parliament ignored their protests as far as the Quartering Act was concerned. In fact, it decided to renew the act each year. In 1767, Parliament passed the Townshend Acts, which taxed tea, glass, paper, lead, and paint imported into the colonies. The colonists, as a way of protest, refused to buy these goods. Soon the Townshend taxes were repealed except for the tax on tea. Even though the tiny tax was only a symbol, it still made the colonists angry.

Boston, as the third largest port in the colonies, was the focus

Colonists burn the hated British tax stamps. Pain understood how the colonists felt about unfair taxes.

of many of these protests. British troops fired into a crowd of protesting men and boys in 1770, killing five and wounding five more. Samuel Adams, a leader of the protesting colonists, condemned this villainy as the Boston Massacre. More protests and riots erupted. On December 16, 1773, some men of Boston disguised as Mohawk Indians boarded British ships and threw all the tea overboard. They called it the Boston Tea Party. When the colonists refused to pay for the destroyed tea, the British Parliament passed the Boston Port Act, which closed Boston Harbor. Parliament also passed a new Quartering Act that could force people to lodge British soldiers in their homes.

These acts of the British Parliament alarmed the people in the other colonies, too. Twelve of the 13 colonies sent delegates to the First Continental Congress. It met in Philadelphia during September and October 1774—a few weeks before Pain arrived in America. The Congress was supposed to discuss the problems and take some sort of action. The First Continental Congress denounced the laws passed by Parliament as violations of the colonists' rights as British subjects. The Congress declared that the Quartering Act and the law closing Boston Harbor were illegal and should not be obeyed. It urged the people of Massachusetts to form a new government to collect taxes. These taxes would be withheld from the royal government until the hated laws were ended. The Congress also suggested that the people arm themselves and form their own militias.

The First Continental Congress decided not to import *any* goods from Britain after December 1, 1774. This ban would stay in effect until the unfair taxes and the Quartering Act were repealed.

Pain understood how the Americans felt. While he was still ill, he wrote a fanciful essay about the ghost of the British hero General James Wolfe appearing to General Thomas Gage, the present governor of Massachusetts who sided with the king, with a warning. "You have come here to deprive your fellow subjects of their liberty." This essay was published in the *Pennsylvania Journal* newspaper on January 4, 1775, and it became the talk of Philadelphia.

By mid-January, Pain was well enough to be out and about the city. He found much to his liking. Thirty thousand people lived there. The streets and sidewalks were paved, clean, and lighted at night thanks to Benjamin Franklin. The city had a police force, firemen, a hospital, an academy for higher education, and seven newspapers.

With Franklin's letters in his pocket, Pain called on Richard Bache. When Bache learned that Pain hoped to open a school, he put him in touch with some wealthy friends. They hired Pain to tutor their sons and paid him well for it. Despite the fact that coming to America had almost cost him his life, Pain felt he was making a good beginning in the New World.

It was not long before Pain found his way to the taverns of Philadelphia. A favorite was the Indian Queen. There he met a printer named Robert Aitken. When Aitken learned that Pain had written the essay about Wolfe and Gage, he told him about the magazine he was starting. Aitken planned to call it the *Pennsylvania Magazine.* He invited Pain to write an introduction in the first issue. He liked Pain's writing and hired him to be the editor. But Aitkens warned Pain not to publish anything that readers might disagree with or that might make them angry.

Pain was paid only £50 a year; nevertheless, it was a job. He took lodgings in a building next to Aitken's print and bookshop and went to work. To be successful, a magazine had to contain a variety of material—some serious, some witty, some practical. Pain wrote much of the material himself and, as editor, accepted or rejected contributions from other writers.

In the March 1775 issue, Pain printed his poem "On the Death of General Wolfe" along with the music the Headstrong Club had made up. It became very popular because Americans had made the young General Wolfe a legend. Although Pain did not sign his own name, he let it be known around the taverns that it was he who really wrote the poem.

In his serious articles, Pain lashed out at dueling as "Gothic [barbarous] and absurd." He made fun of aristocrats' titles: "When I reflect on the pompous titles bestowed on unworthy men, I feel an indignity that instructs me to despise the absurdity."

Those of his articles that could stir up trouble, or at least debate, Pain published in newspapers. His lodgings were across the street from a slave market. What Pain saw there made him sick at heart, and he wrote a fiery article against slavery. He accused Americans of falseness in their charges against England when he asked, why did "they complain so loudly of attempts to enslave them, while they hold so many hundred thousands in slavery; and annually enslave many thousands more, without any pretence of authority, or claim upon them?"

When this essay against slavery was published, a young doctor named Benjamin Rush came to the bookstore seeking Pain. Rush had written an antislavery essay in 1772, but the public reaction against it had hurt his medical practice. As Pain and Rush talked, they found they had more things in common. They were not only both writers, they were both friends of Benjamin Franklin. Within a month after Pain's article appeared, they formed the American Antislavery Society in Philadelphia. Franklin was later named its president.

Both Pain and Rush were stunned by what happened the month after they met. General Thomas Gage in Massachusetts learned that some colonists were stockpiling gunpowder and military supplies in the village of Concord outside Boston. He ordered a surprise march to seize the supplies. Paul Revere, a Boston silversmith, tried to ride from Boston to Lexington and Concord to warn people. (He was able to reach Lexington but was captured before reaching Concord.) The British soldiers got to the town of Lexington in the early morning of April 19, 1775. The Americans were waiting for them with guns in hand. No one knows who fired the first shot, but eight colonists were killed and seven wounded. Only one British soldier was hurt. The British troops marched on to Concord and found the guns the colonists had collected. By this time, news of the deaths at Lexington had spread around the countryside. When the British tried to cross the Connecticut River at a bridge near Concord, farmers and merchants fired on them. They chased the British back to Boston, inflicting casualties on 273 British soldiers. On hearing about this skirmish, both Rush and Pain agreed independence was the only future for America. Rush introduced Pain to other influential men in Philadelphia who were working quietly for independence, too. Pain recognized that the war for independence from Britain had already begun.

British troops retreat from Concord. Such early small battles made it clear to Pain that full-scale war was about to begin.

On May 7, 1775, Franklin returned from England at last. Three days later, the delegates from 12 of the colonies met in Philadelphia for the Second Continental Congress. (Georgia's delegate arrived in September.) Even after Lexington and Concord, the Congress continued to argue about what to do. Most delegates still wanted peace. Back in Great Britain in Parliament, men like Edmund Burke spoke again and again for repeal of the hated laws and taxes. But King George III would not listen to them.

Although no one spoke openly of independence, the Second Continental Congress appointed George Washington as general and commander-in-chief with orders to raise an army. Secretly, the

The Second Continental Congress appointed George Washington to lead the new army to victory against the forces of Great Britian.

Congress formed a Committee of Secret Correspondence. They entered into talks with Britain's ancient enemies, France and Spain, for military aid. Within a year, Silas Deane was sent to France to beg or buy guns, ammunition, and clothing for Washington's army. The colonies could not manufacture enough. Congress also started building a navy and arming privateers. Most important, Congress asked the people of each colony to hold elections and replace the British authorities. Months later, Benjamin Franklin's son, the last royal governor of New Jersey, was arrested.

On June 17, 1775, about 1,500 colonists from New England besieged the British troops who occupied Boston. The British tried to drive them out in the Battle of Bunker Hill. They succeeded only because the Americans ran out of gunpowder and had to retreat. It cost the British 1,000 killed and wounded.

In the July issue of *Pennsylvania Magazine*, Pain published a poem set to music he had written about the Liberty Tree in Boston. The elm in the center of the city had became a symbol of defiance against tyranny. The song caught on in all the colonies.

Despite his success with the magazine, Pain could not get along with his employer, Robert Aitkin. Pain had tripled the number of magazines sold, so he thought he should be paid more money. Aitken refused, saying Pain was lazy and did not get his work done on time. Pain did like to sleep most of the day and talk and drink most of the night. He did not adopt his admired friend Franklin's method of moving up in the world: "Early to bed, and early to rise, makes a man healthy, wealthy, and wise."

Meanwhile, the British were recruiting troops in Canada for an invasion of New York. American forces headed for Montreal and Quebec City to prevent a British invasion from Canada.

In November 1775, word reached Philadelphia that King George III had declared the colonies of Massachusetts, Rhode Island, and Connecticut to be in a state of rebellion. In December, Parliament passed the Prohibitory Act, which resulted in a blockade of American ports. The leaders of the colonists were still in Philadelphia attending the Second Continental Congress. Pain, urged on by Benjamin Rush, decided to write a series of newspaper articles addressed to the American people. He hoped to persuade them to declare themselves independent of England and to

35

do it now. Yet Pain realized that many of the colonists were Englishmen like himself. It would be hard for them to hate their parent country. Instead, he focused their anger against King George III.

Pain began by attacking the whole idea of people being ruled by monarchs. He also attacked the British House of Lords. This was part of the Parliament, the British lawmaking body, but only nobles could sit in the House of Lords. According to Pain, the only good part of the Parliament was the elected part, the House of Commons. But even that body was controlled by the king.

According to Pain, "England, since the conquest [in 1066], hath known some few good monarchs, but groaned beneath a much larger number of bad ones; . . . Of more worth is one honest man to society and in the sight of God, than all the crowned ruffians that ever lived." He strongly favored a republic, the form of government in which citizens vote for their leaders and elect representatives who make the laws and govern according to the laws.

Pain glorified the idea of independence:

> The sun never shined on a cause of greater worth. 'Tis not the affair of a city, a county, a province, or a kingdom, but of a continent—of at least one eighth part of the habitable globe. 'Tis not the concern of a day, a year, or an age; posterity are virtually involved in the contest, and will be more or less affected, even to the end of time, by proceedings now. Now is the seed-time of continental union, faith and honor.

Pain was trying to show the colonists that to declare and fight for independence was not a small battle in an obscure corner of the earth. He had an incredible vision of the effects that American independence would eventually have on the future of the world.

Another focus of his attack was the very idea that England was "the *parent* or *mother country*":

> This new world hath been the asylum for the persecuted lovers of civil and religious liberty from *every part* of Europe. Hither have they fled, not from the

tender embraces of the mother, but from the cruelty of a monster; and so it is true of England, that the same tyranny which drove the emigrants from home, pursues their descendents still. . . . Not one third of the inhabitants, even of this province [Pennsylvania], are of English descent. Wherefore I reprobate [condemn] the phrase of parent or mother country applied to England only, as being false, selfish, narrow and ungenerous.

Pain pointed out the absurdity of the large American colonies being ruled by the comparatively small nation of Britain:

[T]here is something very absurd, in supposing a continent to be perpetually governed by an island. In no instance hath nature made the satellite larger than its primary planet, and as England and America, with respect to each other, reverses the common order of nature, it is evident they belong to different systems; England to Europe, America itself.

Pain presented the advantages the American colonies had. They had forests with tall, straight trees to build their own navy. He was not above appealing to personal greed. "Another reason why the present time is preferable to all others, is, that the fewer our numbers are, the more land there is yet unoccupied." His final appeal was the following:

These proceedings may at first appear strange and difficult; but, like all other steps which we have already passed over, will in a little time become familiar and agreeable; and, until an independence is declared, the Continent will feel itself like a man who continues putting off some unpleasant business from day to day, yet know it must be done, hates to set about it, wishes it over, and is continually haunted with the thoughts of its necessity.

The essay ended with the suggestion that what amounted to a declaration of independence be written. He called for a

> manifesto [official statement] to be published, and despatched [sent] to foreign courts, setting forth the miseries we have endured, and the peaceable methods we have ineffectually used for redress [correcting the problems]: declaring, at the same time, that not being able, any longer, to live happily or safely under the cruel disposition of the British court, we have been driven to the necessity of breaking all connections with her.

What Pain wrote was for everyday people like himself. He knew them; he understood their fears and concerns; he could talk to them in their language. Just plain common sense was what common people lived by. He wanted to lay before them why they and the American colonies needed to be independent. It was a chance no people have ever had before. But without their support, it could never happen.

Rush urged him to have the articles printed up in pamphlet form. Newspapers probably would not dare to run them. But most printers would not be so reckless either, since the printer's name would be stamped on the pamphlet. Printers could have their property seized and be thrown in jail, or worse, for this call to rebellion. Even Pain was not so foolhardy as to sign "Tom Pain" to his work. Instead, he signed it "written by an Englishman." But a printer named Robert Bell believed in independence, too, and he did not care what people thought. He dared to print 1,000 copies, agreeing to split the profits with Pain fifty-fifty.

On January 9, 1776, the pamphlet *Common Sense* went on sale in bookstalls around Philadelphia for two shillings. (For an unskilled worker, two shillings equaled a bit more than one day's wages.) There was no advertisement of the pamphlet in the newspapers because neither Pain nor Bell could afford it. But Pain did place his pamphlet on sale the same day copies of King George's speech to Parliament reached Philadelphia. The king's speech angered many colonists. The king said he would put an end to "a

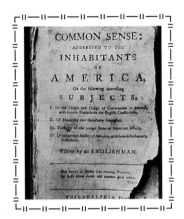

Pain's *Common Sense*
became a huge best-seller.

rebellious war" of the American colonists. The 1,000 copies of *Common Sense* sold out in a week.

Bell wanted to print and rush out another 1,000 copies. When Pain asked him where his share of the profits were from the first 1,000, Bell said there were none. Pain was not hungry for money himself. With his share of the money, he planned to buy mittens to send to Washington's troops trying to take Quebec City. Pain stormed out of Bell's print shop taking *Common Sense* with him.

Pain added more to the next edition of his pamphlet, including a letter to the Quakers, who had come out against independence. They wanted to reach an agreement with Britain for the sake of peace. Pain knew better than to ask them to fight, but he pleaded with them not to support the king. Pain took his pamphlet to two other printers. B. Towne printed 3,000 copies, and Styner and Cist printed 3,000 more. Pain guaranteed their printing costs if they would sell copies for one shilling so more people could afford to buy them. Pain never did make enough to buy mittens for the troops. In fact, he paid out £40 ($180) in printing costs. Pain still did not understand business; he passed up a fortune. However, some men of Philadelphia were impressed by Pain's public spirit. When they learned how poor he was, they sent him $108 so he would not be in debt.

Pain could have been hanged for what he had written. That is why the "great men" spoke of independence among themselves, but not in a public proclamation. Pain was not a wealthy planter like George Washington and Thomas Jefferson. He was not an educated man like Samuel and John Adams and Benjamin Rush. He certainly was not a rich man like Benjamin Franklin and John Hancock. He was a poor man who dared risk the only things he possessed—his life and his liberty—to speak out publicly for the independence of his newly adopted country.

CHAPTER FOUR

The Soldier

om Pain succeeded beyond his wildest dreams. More than 150,000 copies of *Common Sense* were sold in a country of 3,000,000 inhabitants. Printers all over the colonies made copies. It was sent to France and translated. The poor liked it because it denounced kings. The French king liked it because it attacked his enemy, the British king.

For a while, people thought Sam or John Adams or Ben Franklin or Benjamin Rush had written *Common Sense*. When people finally discovered that Pain was the author, he became instantly famous. After nearly 40 years, he had finally succeeded at something. Pain quietly began adding a final "e" to his name.

General George Washington himself read a copy of *Common Sense*. Washington wrote after the British burned Norfolk, Virginia, "A few more of such flaming arguments, as were exhibited at Falmouth and Norfolk, added to the sound doctrine and unanswerable reasoning contained in the pamphlet 'Common Sense,' will not leave numbers at a loss to decide upon the propriety of a separation."

Common Sense, coupled with the king's harsh speech to Parliament, caused American thinking to turn toward independence—at least among some people. Every day more and more members of Congress came out saying they had always been for independence. But people were afraid of the unknown. Most governments throughout the world were monarchies. People had little or no idea of how another kind of government would work. When an election was held for the Pennsylvania State Assembly, most of the candidates supporting independence lost.

At the end of *Common Sense*, Paine had put forth the idea of a "manifesto" of independence. The Second Continental Congress appointed Thomas Jefferson to head a committee with John Adams, Ben Franklin, Robert R. Livingston, and Roger Sherman

40

to draw up the document Paine had suggested. On July 4, 1776, Congress adopted the final draft of the Declaration of Independence. On this occasion, Benjamin Franklin is reported to have said, "Gentlemen, we must now all hang together or we shall most assuredly hang separately."

The Second Continental Congress also appointed a committee to draw up the Articles of Confederation. This was a document that would establish a government and would provide the rules for running it. But Congress did not adopt that for another year and a half.

Common Sense had achieved its goal. Now the states had to

Thomas Jefferson wrote the Declaration of Independence, a document that Paine had suggested in *Common Sense*.

fight to stay independent. Great Britain was not about to let them go quietly out of its empire.

No one believed this "war" could last long. Congress and even Washington asked men to enlist in the army for only three months at a time. They hoped a few thousand volunteers plus state militia would be enough to rid America of the British. After all, England had only 10,000 soldiers in all the colonies including Canada. The Americans had already forced General William Howe to withdraw his troops from Boston and take them to Halifax, Nova Scotia.

Congress also authorized flying camps of 10,000 men. Flying camps were volunteer troops formed for rapid movement from place to place. The men would enlist for a short time and go where they were needed. When the emergency was over, they went home. In July 1776 Paine joined a flying camp being raised in Pennsylvania, Maryland, and Delaware and commanded by Daniel Roberdeau, a rich Philadelphia merchant. Paine was to act as secretary. He refused any pay, asking only for his expenses. The corps marched from Philadelphia to Perth Amboy, New Jersey, and waited. General Washington expected the British to try to capture New York City next.

Sure enough, the British general, Sir Henry Clinton, brought his troops by ship from the southern states to New York in July. General Sir William Howe returned by ship from Halifax with his troops. In August, his older brother, Admiral Lord Richard Howe, brought a fleet and more troops from England. These included about 9,000 Hessian soldiers hired to fight for England. All landed on Staten Island in New York Harbor across a narrow waterway from Perth Amboy. Paine could only watch as ship after ship sailed into New York Bay and unloaded troops until the count reached about 32,000. That was the largest single force the British used in their wars during the 18th century.

The Howe brothers said they were carrying concessions and a plan from the king to reconcile Great Britain and its colonies. Congress appointed a commission headed by Benjamin Franklin to meet with the British on Staten Island. But they learned that the Howe brothers could only offer pardons to those who swore allegiance to the king. The Americans wanted more than that.

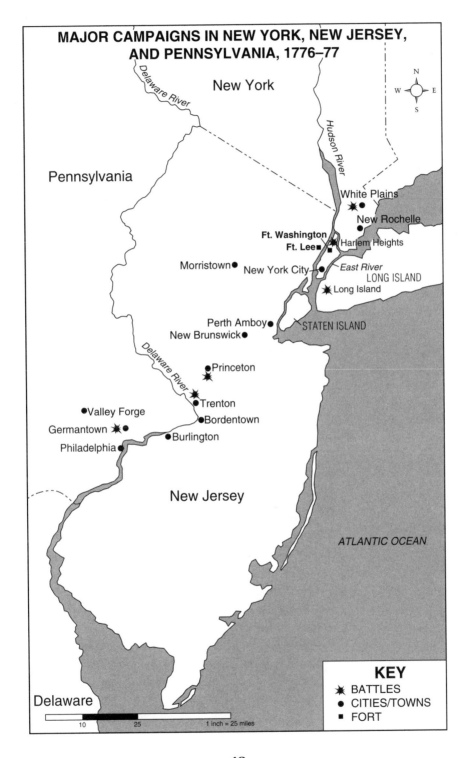

MAJOR CAMPAIGNS IN NEW YORK, NEW JERSEY, AND PENNSYLVANIA, 1776–77

New York

Pennsylvania

Delaware River

Hudson River

White Plains

New Rochelle

Ft. Washington
Ft. Lee ■ Harlem Heights

Morristown ● New York City ─ East River
LONG ISLAND

Long Island

Perth Amboy ●
New Brunswick ●

STATEN ISLAND

Delaware River

Princeton

● Valley Forge

Trenton

Bordentown

Germantown ✸ ●

Philadelphia ● ● Burlington

New Jersey

ATLANTIC OCEAN

Delaware

KEY
✸ BATTLES
● CITIES/TOWNS
■ FORT

10   25   1 inch = 25 miles

Thousands of troops commanded by the British head for Long Island to attack General George Washington's forces.

General Washington knew General Howe could attack in several places. He had no choice but to divide up his few troops, placing one-third on Long Island and one-third in New Jersey. He kept the rest in New York City.

Howe invaded Long Island August 22, 1776. General Washington's men under his direct command put up a brave battle, but over 1,000 were killed or wounded, Paine, as secretary, saw the dispatches from Washington pleading for the flying camp to come to Long Island and help him. But the flying camp refused to leave New Jersey. As a result, General Washington was forced to retreat. Under cover of darkness and fog, he got his men across the East River to the relative safety of New York City on Manhattan Island. The British overran Long Island in less than a week.

The British defeat American troops during the Battle of Long Island.
Washington then led his soldiers in retreat to New York City.

General Washington knew he could not hold New York City against such a superior British force. He wanted to burn it so the British could not use it, but Congress would not let him. Washington decided to withdraw to the northern tip of Manhattan Island called Harlem Heights, where there was high ground and a fort. Another fort, Fort Lee, on the New Jersey side of the Hudson River would prevent British ships from sailing up the river. By September 14, most of New York City had been evacuated. Five thousand men and some cannon remained in the city to fight a delaying action. Another 5,000 men were stationed out along miles of the Manhattan side of the East River to repel the British if they landed there.

Meanwhile, in New Jersey, with their enlistment time finished, the men of the flying camp packed up and went home, Paine collected $48 for his expenses and refused any more. But he did not go back to Philadelphia with the troops. Instead, he hiked up the New Jersey side of the Hudson River to Fort Lee and volunteered his services to General Nathanael Greene. Greene took him on as an aide-de-camp, or assistant, with the rank of brigadier major. Paine also had been hired by the *Philadelphia Journal* newspaper. He was to send back reports on what was happening in the war where Pennsylvania troops were fighting.

On September 15, General Howe started the invasion of Manhattan Island. He landed troops above the city itself to cut off the Americans. When General Washington heard the cannons, he leaped on his horse and rode toward the sound, intending to direct the defenses himself. But halfway there, he met his untrained and undisciplined troops fleeing northward in full retreat. They left scarce equipment like cannons, food, tents, and ammunition behind as each man scrambled to save himself. The British got New York City without a fight.

Major Paine despised the fact that General Greene disobeyed Washington's orders to remove supplies and men not absolutely needed at the forts. General Washington believed that these forts would fall and soon. Supplies were so scarce that he could not afford to lose a single gun. As Washington had predicted, the fort on Harlem Heights surrendered to the British after a fight of only a few hours on November 16. The men had no chance to escape across the Hudson River. Some 2,500 Americans were captured.

Three days later, British troops, under cover of a rainy night, crossed the Hudson River to the west bank six miles north of Fort Lee. Scouts reported the British force had 6,000 to 8,000 men.

The Battle of Harlem Heights, 1776. At the time, Paine was stationed across the Hudson River at Fort Lee.

46

There were only 2,000 or 3,000 Americans at Fort Lee, Paine among them. General Washington himself ordered Fort Lee abandoned and led the men on a double-quick march. The bridge over the Hackensack River was their only means of escape. If the British got there first, the Americans would be cut off and captured.

The troops, including Major Paine, made it across the Hackensack River and stopped in the town of Brunswick much farther south. In that desperate hour, Washington sent a message to General Charles Lee in White Plains, north of New York City. He ordered Lee to leave there with his troops, cross the Hudson River, and reinforce him. General Lee disobeyed orders. No reinforcements came. Washington had only 1,000 men left, and the British and Hessians were in sight. During November and December 1776, General Washington had to lead his troops in retreat across New Jersey and the Delaware River into Pennsylvania.

A few days later, Major Paine was sent to Philadelphia on "public business." He found Congress packing up. Its members were fleeing to Baltimore, Maryland, sure the British would capture Philadelphia, the nation's new capital. No newspapers were being published. The people heard nothing but rumors, most of them false. They were deeply discouraged and frightened. Paine took up his pen to tell the people the truth and give them courage to struggle on:

> These are the times that try men's souls. The summer soldier and the sunshine patriot will, in this crisis, shrink from the service of his country; but he that stands it NOW, deserves the love and thanks of man and woman. Tyranny, like hell, is not easily conquered; yet we have this consolation with us, that the harder the conflict, the more glorious the triumph. What we obtain too cheap, we esteem too lightly: 'tis dearness only that gives everything its value.

Paine laid out the desperate circumstances all would find themselves in if the war failed, and he cried out for support. "I

The *American* CRISIS.

NUMBER I.

By the Author of COMMON SENSE.

THESE are the times that try men's souls: The summer soldier and the sunshine patriot will, in this crisis, shrink from the service of his country; but he that stands it NOW, deserves the love and thanks of man and woman. Tyranny, like hell, is not easily conquered; yet we have this consolation with us, that the harder the conflict, the more glorious the triumph. What we obtain too cheap, we esteem too lightly:—'Tis dearness only that gives every thing its value. Heaven knows how to set a proper price upon its goods; and it would be strange indeed, if so celestial an article as FREEDOM should not be highly rated. Britain, with an army to enforce her tyranny, has declared, that she has a right (*not only to* TAX, but) "*is* "BIND *us in* ALL CASES WHATSOEVER," and if being *bound in that manner* is not slavery, then is there not such a thing as slavery upon earth. Even the expression is impious, for so unlimited a power can belong only to GOD.

WHETHER the Independence of the Continent was declared too soon, or delayed too long, I will not now enter into as an argument; my own simple opinion is, that had it been eight months earlier, it would have been much better. We did not make a proper use of last winter, neither could we, while we were in a dependent state. However, the fault, if it were one, was all our own; we have none to blame but ourselves*. But no great deal is lost yet; all that Howe has been doing for this month past is rather a ravage than a conquest, which the spirit of the Jersies a year ago would have quickly repulsed, and which time and a little resolution will soon recover.

I have as little superstition in me as any man living, but my

* "The present winter" (meaning the last) "is worth an "age, if rightly employed, but if lost, or neglected, the whole "Continent will partake of the evil; and there is no punish- "ment that man does not deserve, be he who, or what, or "where he will, that may be the means of sacrificing a season "so precious and useful." COMMON SENSE.

Paine's *The American Crisis,* was the first of a number of *Crisis* pamphlets.

call not upon a few, but upon all: not on *this* state or *that* state, but on *every* state; up and help us; lay your shoulders to the wheel; better have too much force than too little, when so great an object is at stake." He signed it "Common Sense."

He entitled his essay the *American Crisis* because the country and independence itself were in crisis. It appeared in the *Pennsylvania Journal* on December 19, 1776, and in pamphlet form a few days later. Major Thomas Paine took copies back to General George Washington. It was read to all the troops, and it helped to lift their spirits as well as those of the people at home.

Philadelphia sent men to help General Washington protect the city. General Lee's army without Lee (who had been captured) found their way to Washington's camp. The American troops of General Horatio Gates arrived from Canada. A desperate Congress granted Washington full authority to conduct the war as he saw fit. Only a man of Washington's strong character could have resisted abusing this power handed to him. A lesser man might have set himself up as a dictator or even king with a ready army to back him up. Instead, Washington used his power wisely.

Even though his soldiers had increased in numbers, most of the present enlistments would be up by December 31. Washington had to do something or the war for independence would be over.

Three thousand Hessian soldiers were at the small town of Trenton, east of the Delaware River. Washington planned to take it. On Christmas night, Washington had three groups of his men cross the Delaware by boat at three different points. He led one group himself.

But spies were everywhere. A British soldier at Princeton sent a letter to the Hessian commander at Trenton telling him the Americans would attack Christmas night. A small party of Americans had been sent across the river to scout by a commander who did not know of Washington's plan. Hessians, out on patrol, met these Americans and chased them off. Thinking this was the American force they had been warned about, they returned to Trenton and continued celebrating Christmas.

While Washington's troops were crossing the Delaware River, a blizzard began. Without his knowledge, the two other groups of soldiers turned back without sending him word. Not knowing he

George Washington's troops prepare to cross the Delaware River on Christmas night, 1776.

would have no support, Washington and his troops pushed on through the storm. The Hessian commander at Trenton was so sure no one would attack on such a night, that he did not post sentries. Washington's army appeared out of the whirling snow and took the Hessians by complete surprise. With hardly a shot fired, 1,000 of the enemy troops surrendered. None of the Americans were killed.

Washington wanted to press on to capture the next town, Burlington. But his officers persuaded him to take the prisoners back across the Delaware. They also wanted to protect six pieces of artillery, 1,000 guns, and other much needed captured equipment. Washington agreed he could not ask more of his exhausted men when they had performed so well.

But Washington needed to strike again before the enlistments were up. He recrossed the Delaware on December 29 and led his troops back to Trenton, which the Hessians had abandoned. In fact, they had abandoned most of New Jersey. But the British were on the march from Princeton 12 miles away to catch General Washington and his troops this time. The two armies met. Washington held one side of Trenton; the British held the other with a creek between them. It was dark by now, and the British decided to camp for the night and fight the battle in the morning. Not Washington! He used the cover of darkness to remove his troops and capture Princeton.

Paine described the event this way:

> General Washington, the better to cover and disguise his retreat from Trenton, had ordered a line of fires to be lighted up in front of his camp. These not only served to give an appearance of going to rest, and continuing that deception, but they effectually concealed from the British whatever was acting behind them, for flame can no more be seen through than a wall, and in this situation, it may with propriety be said, they became a pillar of fire to one army, and a pillar of cloud to the other. After this, by a circuitous march of about eighteen miles, the Americans reached Princeton early in the morning.

Washington at the Battle of Princeton. It lasted less than an hour, but 400 British troops were killed, wounded, or taken prisoner.

When the British in Trenton woke up and discovered what had happened, they were in hot pursuit. But that pursuit was slowed by the fact that the Americans had burned all the bridges behind them. When the British came in sight, Washington had to leave behind the useful arms he had found. The army did take new blankets and marched off with several hundred more prisoners. General Washington wanted to march north and take the town of Brunswick near Perth Amboy and the British supplies there. He believed such a victory might end the war. But his men had been up for two nights and a day, and Brunswick was a long march; they could not fight any more.

General Washington did not recross the Delaware again. Over

a period of days, he marched his troops to winter quarters in the mountains around Morristown, New Jersey. The British went back to New York City to lick their wounds.

In winter quarters, Major Paine was not needed. He returned to Philadelphia and described the victories he had witnessed. The country turned from despair to hope.

On January 13, 1777, Paine published *Crisis Number II*. It was an open letter to General Howe. Not that Paine expected Howe would ever see it. It was a piece of propaganda for the American people. It ridiculed Howe, scared the Tories as the Americans who sided with the British were called, and belittled the king. "I laugh at your notion of conquering America. Because you lived in a little country, where an army might run over the whole in a few days, and where a single company of soldiers might put a multitude to the rout, you expected to find it the same here." Then Paine's dream of a revolution some day in England came out when he said, "I, who know England and the disposition of the people well, am confident, that it is easier for us to effect a revolution there, than you a conquest here."

On April 19, he published his *Crisis Number III*. Again he argued persuasively why America should be independent. Remaining attached to England would only drag America into Britain's many wars, especially those against France and Spain. He then reviewed the history that had passed in the two years following Lexington and Concord. He denounced Tories, Quakers, and all who did not support the American cause for independence. "The only road to *peace, honor* and *commerce,* is Independence."

CHAPTER FIVE

The Deane Affair

On March 12, 1777, Congress returned to Philadelphia from Baltimore. One of the first pieces of legislation members of Congress passed was to change the Committee for Secret Correspondence into the more public Committee for Foreign Affairs. John Adams nominated Thomas Paine to be secretary of the committee. General Daniel Roberdeau, Paine's commander in the flying camp and a delegate to Congress, spoke highly of Paine. The nomination was confirmed.

Thomas Paine, the secretary of the Committee for Foreign Affairs.

Paine was flabbergasted when the job was offered to him. He considered it a great honor—more of an honor than it really was. He was only a clerk. But the salary was a good one—$70 a month. Paine's duties were to take minutes of committee meetings and file papers. All this would take Paine only a few hours a day. He would still have time to write for the war effort, which is what Adams and his friends wanted. There was one important restriction. Paine had to swear he would keep everything he saw or heard relating to the committee secret.

In addition to his new job, Thomas Paine remained a major in the Continental Army. All summer long, British General William Howe in New York

53

had kept General Washington guessing as to where he was going to attack. North into New England? West through New Jersey? Or south to try to take the capital, Philadelphia? Finally, in late August 1777, General Howe loaded his troops onto ships in New York. He headed for Philadelphia by way of Chesapeake Bay. General Washington, with no sea power, could not harass him.

Washington marched overland. At dawn on September 11, he had his troops and cannons in place to make a stand against the British at Brandywine Creek, a few miles southwest of Philadelphia. But the British attacked and outmaneuvered the Americans. The Americans retreated—again. As they had done with New York City, the British could now march into Philadelphia without much of a fight.

The Battle of Brandywine Creek was close enough to the city so that Paine could hear the roar of the cannons from his office. Learning during the night of the American defeat at Brandywine, he immediately went to work writing *Crisis Number IV*. Paine proposed that the citizens of Philadelphia defend it: "Gentlemen of the city and country, it is in your power, by a spirited improvement of the present circumstance, to turn it to a real advantage. Howe is now weaker than before, and every shot will contribute to reduce him." By noon the next day, Paine had the short essay completed. He rushed it to a printer, ordering that 4,000 copies be turned out and given away at his own expense. Then he went to General Thomas Mifflin, who was in the city. Paine pleaded with him to take command of the city's defenses. Mifflin said he was too ill, then hightailed it out of town.

Congress fled, too. On September 19, 1777, Paine packed up all the papers belonging to the Committee for Foreign Affairs. He sent them by a small boat up the Delaware River to safety at Trenton just as British troops entered Philadelphia.

Paine escaped from the city and went in search of General Nathanael Greene and the main army. Finding the army was not easy. Washington was moving them about every day to avoid a trap by General Howe. Paine arrived at General Greene's headquarters October 3, as the army was preparing for the Battle of Germantown north of Philadelphia. General Washington needed a victory—another Trenton and Princeton—before winter to

Thomas Paine could hear the sounds of the fighting at the Battle of Brandywine Creek as he worked in his office in Philadelphia.

revive the spirits of his soldiers and the American public. Greene ordered Major Paine to remain in camp during the night before the battle. The rest of the American army moved into position to attack at dawn.

Paine set out at five the next morning for the battle. As he met wounded coming back, he was told the British were retreating. But a few miles farther on he met a friend, Colonel Owen Biddle. He warned Paine to turn back or he would be captured. How the Americans snatched defeat from the jaws of what seemed certain victory that day not even General Washington could explain. There was a heavy fog. The Americans could not see and began firing at each other. This caused confusion. When in doubt, the poorly trained Americans usually retreated, every man for himself. They did not wait for commands from their officers. Although this made for poor warfare, it saved many lives and so enabled the soldiers to fight another day.

Two days after the Battle of Germantown, General Washington sent Paine with messages to Fort Mifflin and Fort Mercer on the Delaware River downstream from Philadelphia. The boat Paine used was fired on by British cannons as it sneaked past the city now occupied by the British. When he got to Fort Mifflin, two British cannons shelled the fort. Soon the Americans had to evacuate these two forts. With their loss, the British now had control of the Delaware River south of Philadelphia. Paine volunteered to take four or five men down the Delaware and set fire to the British fleet. But this dangerous plan was vetoed.

Paine rode with General Greene's troops on other missions to harass the British around Philadelphia. But they were unable to accomplish anything. In December, General Washington finally led his army into winter quarters at Valley Forge, northwest of Philadelphia. Paine sadly watched the soldiers, some barefoot and without coats in the cold and snow, build the crude huts they would inhabit over the winter of 1777-78.

By now, Congress had gathered at the rural town of York, Pennsylvania, safely west of the broad Susquehanna River. In January 1778, Paine went there to resume his duties as secretary to the Committee for Foreign Affairs. But there was little for him to do since only 15 to 20 delegates to Congress were present. The rest had gone home. Paine decided to spend the winter in the larger city of Lancaster, Pennsylvania, where many refugees from Philadelphia were living. He was invited to stay at the home of William Henry, a wealthy gunsmith and scientist.

During that winter, Paine wrote *Crisis Number V.* It was in two parts. The first part was directed at General Howe. Paine described Howe's military victories: "They resemble the labors of a puppy pursuing his tail; the end is still at the same distance, and all the turnings round must be done over again." In the second part, he spoke to the "Inhabitants of America." He encouraged them to support a large army by a draft, if necessary. He wrote: "The only way to finish a war with the least possible bloodshed, or perhaps without any, is to collect an army, against the power of which the enemy shall have no chance. By not doing this, we prolong war, and double both calamities and the expenses of it." The third purpose of *Crisis Number V* was to support Washington. Paine had learned there was a plot to replace Washington with General Horatio Gates. Gates had won a great victory at Saratoga, New York, in October 1777, while Washington was losing at Brandywine and Germantown. In *Crisis Number V,*

Paine made every defeat sound like part of General Washington's grand plan for victory.

Paine had suggested in *Common Sense* in 1776 that France and probably Spain would come to the aid of the colonies if they were independent. In October of that year, Benjamin Franklin had returned to Europe. With the help of two other Americans, Silas Deane and Arthur Lee, he persuaded the French it was to their advantage to help the United States against England. In the early months of 1778, France signed an alliance treaty with the United States. In it, France recognized the United States as an independent country and promised money and military aid. France had already been sending arms and money secretly for a year through the efforts of Silas Deane.

With the Treaty of Alliance, the British expected the French would soon send troops and ships to America. Without a shot being fired, the British abandoned Philadelphia in June 18, 1778, and retreated to New York City again to build a stronger defense.

Congress returned to Philadelphia in July, just in time to greet the new French ambassador to the United States, Conrad Gérard. He was accompanied by Silas Deane, whom Congress had recalled from France.

From Europe, Arthur Lee had written to his brother Richard Henry Lee in Congress. Arthur Lee said he suspected Silas Deane

The Americans and the French sign their 1778 Treaty of Amity and Commerce and Treaty of Alliance.

was personally profiting from the sale of military supplies from France to the United States. When a bill arrived for millions of dollars for French military equipment, Congress became alarmed.

Silas Deane was called before Congress, but it was impossible for Congress to get to the truth. Deane had left his account books in France. He had had to work with Frenchmen who set up fake companies. Supplies were often sent to America by way of the French West Indies in the Caribbean. All these strategies had to be carried on to maintain secrecy because France was at peace with Britain. If it ever became known publicly that the French had been helping the United States even *before* the treaty was signed, it would cause great embarrassment for France. It might even lead France into a war with Britain, possibly other countries as well.

To continue the secrecy, Congress conducted its investigation of Deane in closed sessions. When Congress refused to let Deane speak in his own defense, he wrote a letter to the newspapers complaining of his treatment. This led to a public clamor against Congress.

But no one in Congress answered Deane's charges publicly in the newspapers, so Thomas Paine took it upon himself to do it. From the papers Paine saw as part of his work as secretary to the Committee for Foreign Affairs, he was convinced that Deane was guilty. Paine showed what he had written to friends. They *all* advised him not to publish it. But Paine ignored their good advice and had it printed anyway. It was a rather mild rebuke to Deane. Paine did not accuse Deane of anything except not using good judgment. Much to Paine's surprise, the public and Congress started attacking *him*. A bully in the street pushed him into the gutter. Letters against him appeared in the press. Paine fought back with a series of newspaper articles. He used facts to prove his point. But that information was from the papers of the Committee for Foreign Affairs, which he had sworn to keep secret.

Paine had stirred up real trouble this time. The French ambassador Gérard was furious at this embarrassment to his country. Fearing the loss of French help, Congress forced Paine to

Silas Deane meets Lafayette. Thomas Paine made many political enemies when he disclosed secret information about Deane.

resign. On January 16, 1779, they voted to accept Paine's resignation, although it was a tie vote. The anti-Deane supporters voted against accepting Paine's resignation; the pro-Deane faction voted for the resignation. In addition, Congress sent a letter of apology to Gérard stating that France had never sent supplies to the United States before the alliance treaty was signed. Although it was a lie and everyone knew it, such was the way of world diplomacy.

The loss of his job without so much as a hearing broke Thomas Paine's heart. He had been so proud of his position as secretary. (For years afterward, Paine signed his important writing, "Secretary for Foreign Affairs to Congress in the American war.") He refused to leave his room or see anyone for four months.

Although isolating himself, Paine continued to write. He defended his honor, which, he claimed, Congress had tried to take from him in a secret, unjust manner. For six months, he sent letters to the Congress asking for a hearing to explain his actions. Paine thought he had betrayed no secrets because by June 1778 England and France were at war again, anyway. Through most of 1779, Paine was attacked in the press by persons too cowardly to sign their names. His life was made miserable.

As for Silas Deane, Congress did not punish him, but they no longer employed him. He returned to Europe where he soon was working for the British government. Deane's former supporters, among them Robert Morris and Gouverneur Morris, admitted they had been duped. Paine was eventually vindicated.

Colonel Owen Biddle, who saved Paine from capture at the Battle of Germantown, gave him a job as an ordinary clerk in his store. At least it allowed Paine to earn enough to keep a roof over his head and to eat.

All the stress and living in such poverty took its toll on Thomas Paine's health. In August 1779 he fell ill with a fever that lasted until October. He decided to leave the United States and go to France, but he had no money to pay his passage. Paine wrote a letter to the president of the Pennsylvania Assembly. He wanted to write a history of the war and asked for money to support himself while he was writing it. Instead, the Pennsylvania Assembly did something better, they gave him a job. On November 2, 1779, Thomas Paine was appointed clerk to the Pennsylvania Assembly. His spirits lifted, and he eagerly set to work. One of the first pieces of legislation he worked on was an antislavery bill. Paine is believed to have written the preamble, that is, the introduction to it. The Pennsylvania Assembly passed the antislavery law in March 1780.

By 1780, not only France, but Spain, Holland, Russia, Denmark, and Sweden were at war with England. But this did not help the United States much. Washington reported that his troops at Morristown, New Jersey, had spent another bad winter.

A severe storm crossed New York and New Jersey in January bringing six to eight feet of snow. The troops could not get out and search for food. By spring, rations were cut to one-eighth the normal amount, and the troops had not been paid. Some had even mutinied, and Washington could not blame them. This time the army's suffering was not the fault of the British, but of the states and Congress. The Articles of Confederation had not been ratified by all states yet. The United States had no official central government. Each state drafted its own constitution and was more or less independent of the others. Congress had no power to impose taxes. It had been paying for the war by printing money, but that money had become worthless. The states were supposed to provide Congress with money and supplies to support the Continental Army. But the states rarely met their assigned share of the costs. The United States of America was in economic collapse.

Washington wrote a letter to the Pennsylvania Assembly. "The crisis, in every point of view, is extraordinary; and extraordinary expedients are necessary." He pleaded with them to contribute their state's quota of money and supplies to the Continental Army. Paine read it aloud to the members of the Pennsylvania lawmaking body. This was followed by terrible news. On May 12, 1780, the British had captured Charleston, South Carolina, and about 5,000 American soldiers. It was the worst American defeat of the war. Paine wrote *Crisis Number IX*. He tried to make the people see the fall of Charleston as a victory:

> Afflicting as the loss of Charleston may be, yet if it universally rouse us from the slumber of twelve months past, and renew in us the spirit of former days, it will produce an advantage more important than its loss. America ever *is* what she *thinks* herself to be.

To help General Washington and the army, Paine wrote letters to several wealthy men. He called upon them to give money to support the war effort. He reminded them if the war was lost, they would have the most to lose. He gave $500 of his own money to get the plan started—practically all he had. The men he wrote to liked the idea and immediately called a meeting of Philadelphia's business leaders. Soon about $1,350,000 was raised. To take care of the money, the Bank of Pennsylvania was established, the first bank in the United States.

The money collected by the merchants, however, was not enough to meet the expenses of the government or to continue the war. Paine suggested that France be asked for more money, a million or more now and additional money every year until the war was won. When Paine talked to men he knew in Congress, they thought it was worth a try.

Colonel John Laurens—an aide to Washington—was appointed "Envoy Extraordinary to France." He was the son of Henry Laurens, the former president of the Congress. Laurens, although well educated in Europe, charming, and brave, was also young—only 26. He asked to have Paine appointed as secretary to help him deal with the French government. But Congress objected to Paine's being the official secretary. These would be delicate discussions, and Paine had proved he could not keep secrets. Thomas Paine offered to accompany Laurens as unofficial secretary, paying his own way.

Laurens and Paine could not leave the United States from Philadelphia because the British had it blockaded. The two men had to travel 300 miles to Boston. They set sail on the *Alliance* on February 11, 1781. Five days out at sea they were thrown out of their bunks one night when the ship hit an iceberg. Paine and Laurens dashed on deck to find themselves surrounded by ice and in the midst of a storm. Part of the deck was torn away when the ship sideswiped another iceberg. It was a terrifying night; not until morning was the ship in open water again.

The *Alliance* was also a privateer. When Captain John Berry saw the sail and flag of a British ship, he gave chase, only to have the larger ship turn and chase him. All men were armed, and Colonel Laurens was put in command to repulse a boarding party—if it came to that. The *Alliance* escaped. But the next day, it chased more ships, captured a British cutter, and freed a ship belonging to a neutral country.

The *Alliance* made port in 23 days at L'Orient, France. Much to Thomas Paine's surprise, he found that his writings had made him famous in France. The mayors of towns turned out to greet him as he and Laurens traveled from the coast to Paris.

Benjamin Franklin introduced Laurens and Paine to "great men" in the French government. These Frenchmen, in turn, were honored to meet the great Thomas Paine. With Franklin's help and Paine's prestige behind him, Laurens was given two ships' worth of supplies and $5 million.

As Laurens was preparing to return home, Paine announced he was staying in France. The French admired him, the Americans did not. Paine was still angry at Congress, especially after the last insult of not appointing him official secretary on this mission to France. He did not want to live in the United States any more. In fact, he had resigned as secretary to the Pennsylvania Assembly before he left. Laurens pleaded with Paine to return, saying he could not handle all the supplies and money alone. Paine reconsidered because he felt sorry for his young friend.

They sailed June 1 on the French naval frigate *Resolu*. The crossing took 84 days. Again, they had to use the port of Boston instead of Philadelphia.

This meant all the supplies and money had to be transported 300 miles back to Philadelphia. Laurens and Paine collected 16 wagons, teams of horses and oxen, and armed guards. Although he was escorting millions in silver, Paine arrived back in Philadelphia without a single dollar in his pocket.

CHAPTER SIX

Rewards

The American victory at the Battle of Saratoga in October 1777 was the turning point in the war. But the fighting continued for another four years. During 1778 and 1779, American troops fought the British and their American Indian allies on the western frontiers. There were major campaigns in the southern states during the years from 1778 through 1781.

The last great battle of the Revolutionary War was fought in October 1781 at Yorktown, Virginia. With the help of French troops and a French fleet, General Washington lay siege to the British general Charles Cornwallis's troops for three weeks. On October 19, at 2:00 P.M., 7,247 soldiers and 820 sailors, one-fourth of all the British troops in North America, laid down their arms and were taken prisoner.

General Charles Cornwallis surrenders to General George Washington at Yorktown, Virginia, in 1781.

Most of the American people, the army, the states, and the Congress thought the war was over. They ignored the king's speech that he was determined to continue the fight. But General Washington knew the war could still be lost. Small battles were being fought in the southern states. He wrote hundreds of letters cautioning the states and the Congress, but few heeded his warning.

In early December, Washington received a letter from Thomas Paine. Since returning from France in August, Paine had been living on small loans from friends. He had offered his services to Congress, but they had not been accepted. He could not seem to find work elsewhere.

General Washington sympathized with Paine's plight. He wrote to Robert Morris, superintendent of finance for Congress, and to Robert R. Livingston, secretary for foreign affairs, seeking some help for Paine. Washington, through most of the war, had wanted someone to write favorable newspaper articles about the army. With the victory at Yorktown and everyone mistakenly thinking the war was all but over, Washington needed this more than ever. Morris thought Paine could help the United States government by writing articles on the importance of taxation and stronger government. Washington, Morris, and Livingston signed a contract with Paine in February 1782 to write for them. He would be paid $800 a year, the money coming from a secret congressional fund. They impressed upon Paine that these payments must remain a secret. Even though Paine needed the money in the worst way, he balked. He had always prided himself that his pen could not be bought. Morris assured him he would only write about what he truly believed in. Paine flattered himself that the cause of liberty would falter without him.

Paine immediately set to work. In *Crisis Number X* he warned America against thinking the war was over. "But let not America wrap herself up in delusive hope and suppose the business done." Paine roused the people to support the war by paying their taxes. He urged the states to meet their quotas of supplying the army with men, goods, and money. He even spelled out what each state should pay according to their population—a combined total of $8 million a year from all the states.

Paine appealed to people's pocketbooks; he pointed out that if there was money in the United States Treasury, paper currency would be worth something again.

He warned that terrible atrocities would happen to Americans if the British were allowed to win:

> [O]mit or delay no one preparation necessary to secure the ground which we so happily stand upon. . . . I consider the war of America against Britain as the country's war, the public's war, or the war of the people in their own behalf, for the security of their natural rights and the protection of their own property.

On the other side, the British were getting tired of the war. They were embarrassed that their finely trained troops could not put down the spirit of the Americans and crush Washington's ragtag army. In addition, the French had won a number of battles against the British in the West Indies in 1781 and early 1782. On February 27, 1782, Parliament voted to start peace talks. This made King George III so angry that he threatened to abdicate, that is, to give up his position of king. He warned Britain would collapse if the colonies were set free. Nevertheless, leaders in Parliament who supported continuing the war were outvoted. A different parliamentary group, which opposed the war, came to power. They decided to start direct talks with the Americans.

On November 30, 1782, a preliminary peace treaty was signed. On April 19, 1783, the eighth anniversary of Lexington and Concord, Paine published his final paper in the *Crisis* series, *Crisis Number XIII*. As if to come full circle, he began with the words from the first *Crisis,* which he had written in the dark days of 1776. "'The times that tried men's souls' are over—and the greatest and completest revolution the world ever knew, is gloriously and happily accomplished." His work for independence was finished at last. Now what?

Paine's greatest concern was money. The agreement with Washington, Morris, and Livingston ended with the war. Robert Morris suggested that he appeal to Congress for a pension. Paine got a letter off to Congress June 7, 1783. Congress referred it to a committee that set up an appointment with him to discuss it. But the request for a pension was forgotten when mutinous Pennsylvania troops marched on Philadelphia and surrounded the State House where Congress was meeting. The troops demanded months of back pay. Congress fled to Princeton, New Jersey. Members of Congress blamed Pennsylvania for not protecting them from its own militia! When Congress did not return to Philadelphia, Paine published a paper urging it to come back. The document was signed by over 1,000 important citizens. Congress was not impressed and remained for the time being in Princeton. Nothing was done about Paine's request for money. Actually, there was nothing Congress could do about money. The soldiers had not been paid. The national debt was mounting daily, and Congress had no money to pay even the interest. Under the Articles of Confederation, finally put into effect in 1781, all 13 states had to approve any revenues-raising measure Congress passed or the measure was dead. All 13 states seldom could agree on anything.

Robert Morris suggested that Paine write to Congress again. This time he should carefully lay out in detail and supply supporting documents showing what he had done to aid the cause for independence. General Washington, who had moved his headquarters to Rocky Hill, New Jersey, to guard Congress and await the final signed peace treaty, invited Paine to visit him:

Rocky Hill, Sept. 10, 1783

I have learned since I have been at this place, that you are at Bordentown. Whether for the sake of retirement or economy, I know not. Be it for either, for both, or whatever it may, if you will come to this place, and partake with me, I shall be exceedingly happy to see you.

Your presence may remind Congress of your past services to this country; and if it is in my power to impress them, command my best exertions with freedom, as they will be rendered cheerfully by one, who entertains a lively sense of the importance of

your works, and who, with much pleasure, sub-
scribes himself,

Your sincere friend, G. Washington

Paine was at Bordentown, New Jersey, at the home of his
friend Colonel Joseph Kirkbride when he received this letter.
Paine was recovering from scarlet fever. When he was finally well
enough to visit Rocky Hill, he and Washington spent the days
talking of many things. A subject they had in common was an
interest in science. Washington had heard that the water on a
nearby creek could be set on fire. One night they tried an experi-
ment. They set out in a small boat on the creek. As soldiers stirred
up the mud on the bottom, bubbles came to the surface.
Washington set a roll of paper on fire and threw it over the side of
the boat. The surface of the water burst into flames. (This may
have been methane gas.)

A few days later the official Treaty of Paris ending the
Revolutionary War reached Princeton. It had been signed in Paris
on September 3, 1783. Benjamin Franklin, John Jay of New York,
and John Adams had worked two years to secure it. The last of
the British troops left New York City on November 25, 1783.
Washington rode into the city in triumph at last. Paine accompanied him.

While Paine was in New York, he met James Duane, a delegate
to Congress from New York. Duane told him Congress had buried
his appeal for a pension in a file. Duane suggested that Paine
apply to the individual states to recognize his services. Under
Duane's instructions, Paine wrote a letter to the New York
Assembly. He sent with it a copy of the paper he had submitted to
Congress listing his many services to the cause of the Revolution.

Thomas Paine gave a boost to his fame at this time. He wrote
and published in December 1783 *A Supernumerary Crisis*. In it,
he condemned Britain for not allowing American ships to trans-
port American goods to Caribbean ports and conduct trade
there. The war was over. But the British boldly stated, "'It will be a
long time before American states can be brought to act as a
nation, neither are they to be feared as such by us.'" Paine used
this insult to present a forceful reason for a strong union of the

George Washington enters New York City after the British leave in November 1783. Paine soon urged a strong government be set up.

states. He argued, "United, she [the United States] is formidable, . . . separated, she is a medley of individual nothings, subject to the sport of foreign nations."

Paine was still struggling for money to live on. With the additional help of letters from George Washington, Robert Morris, and Robert R. Livingston, in April 1784, New York State presented Paine with a 277-acre farm and house in New Rochelle worth $4,000. Paine was very pleased. He rented out to tenants the farm and house plus 400 more acres he had purchased. Paine was then able to live on the income.

Appealing to the state legislatures had worked so well that Paine used the large gift from New York as an example for other states. Again, Washington helped him. He wrote to the Pennsylvania Assembly, which had once employed Paine. A year later, Pennsylvania gave him $2,250. Paine thought it was stingy, not nearly what he should have received. It was, however, more

New York State presented Thomas Paine with a 277-acre farm and house in New Rochelle as a reward for his work during the war.

than the average skilled craftsman in Philadelphia earned in five or six years.

In October, Congress awarded Paine $3,000, but he was disappointed. It was not the $6,000 he had asked for to cover the expenses since coming to America. He figured that Congress still owed him back salary for his work as secretary to the Foreign Affairs Committee. But this was all Paine was going to get. After Congress gave him the money, the states did not feel they had to do more. The almost $10,000 he received in money and property was a rather large amount for the times.

One of his wealthy friends gave him a horse, Button, the first he had owned since his last one was sold at auction in Lewes, England. Paine purchased a small house and five acres of land in Bordentown near his good friend Colonel Joseph Kirkbride. Bordentown was just up the Delaware River from Philadelphia and a day or two's journey from New York City. Franklin had returned to Philadelphia on September 14, 1785, and Paine visited him often. Paine as well as Robert Morris, Gouverneur Morris, and Benjamin Rush were members of Franklin's Society for Political Inquiries. They met in Franklin's home to discuss politics and science.

But Thomas Paine felt he was finished with politics. No longer did he have to write for a living. He could turn to his other love— science.

He had had an idea for some time that Americans needed bridges to cross their many rivers. Bridges would allow easier and faster travel and expansion westward. But the bridges of the United States could not be like the bridges of Europe. Many of the rivers in North America froze in winter, and the powerful force of ice moving downstream could take out bridge supports. He had seen that happen in the Delaware River, which flowed near his house. Paine envisioned a single-span arched bridge made in sections like a spider's web. The ends would rest on the banks of a river for support, not on piers in the river. It would be made of iron, not wood or stones. This was a revolutionary idea.

Paine hired John Hall, a carpenter-mechanic recently arrived from England, to help him. In a workshop in Bordentown, they built a wooden model and tested it. Then they built one of iron. Paine interested Franklin in the bridge. Franklin allowed Paine to put the models in his own garden in Philadelphia where people could come, look at them, and try them.

On New Year's Day 1787, the bridge models were moved to the Pennsylvania State House and exhibited. The bridge had 13 sections in honor of the 13 states. Each section could be prefabricated at an iron forge and then put in place, instead of having workers build the bridge on site. The Pennsylvania Assembly was considering building a bridge over the Schuykill River in Philadelphia. A committee was appointed to study Paine's invention. But they rejected it for two reasons. Paine estimated the cost would be over $300,000. That was more money than Pennsylvania's whole budget for a year. The other reason was that his plan for a single 400-foot span across the Schuykill was too new an idea on which to risk so much money.

Franklin told Paine he should take the bridge to Europe and

get it approved by the great scientific societies there—the Royal Society in London and the Academy of Sciences in Paris, France. Again Franklin supplied him with many letters to his important friends in France and England.

This time Paine had the money to finance the trip. He had another reason for going, too. Now that the war was over, he received letters from his father. Since it was safe for Thomas Paine to be in England without risk of being arrested for treason, he wanted to see his parents again.

He set sail from New York for France on April 26, 1787, the model of his bridge in the hold of the ship.

CHAPTER SEVEN

Outlawed

A month after leaving New York in April 1787, Paine arrived at Le Havre, France. Just as when he came to America in 1774, he found "the country, into which I had just put my foot, was set on fire about my ears." Again, he had sailed into a revolution.

European nations had been almost constantly at war since the fall of the Roman Empire. France and England had had so many wars everyone but historians had lost count. These wars caused great debts to pile up in all countries. In France, over one-half of the annual budget went to pay the interest on the war debts. France's participation in the American Revolutionary War had created an especially huge war debt. As a result, the government increased taxes on those who could least afford it—the poor people. The churches and the rich nobles did not pay most taxes. French soldiers returning from the American Revolution had seen what the Americans did when they felt they were being taxed unfairly by Great Britain. They revolted.

Even the king of France, Louis XVI, saw that the government could not bleed any more money from the poor. He tried to tax the rich nobles. In the name of "liberty," they refused to be taxed, saying that they had traditional rights not to be taxed. That started a wave of protests across the country.

The middle class of merchants, lawyers, bankers, and business people resented having to pay the high taxes. They also demanded political rights and so at first helped lead the protests.

But Thomas Paine did not concern himself with politics when he arrived in France. He was interested only in his bridge. After reaching Paris, he wasted no time using the letters of introduction Franklin had given him. He became acquainted with important people who could help him such as the French nobleman, the Marquis de Lafayette, who had fought in the American Revolution and had become a great hero. Thomas Jefferson, the

Louis XVI. His government was struggling with debts caused partly by the military costs of helping the Americans fight the British.

United States minister (ambassador) to France at the time, was a great admirer of Paine. Much of what Jefferson had written in the Declaration of Independence was based on Paine's ideas in *Common Sense.* Jefferson was also a scientist and inventor. The two men became good friends in Paris.

With the help of his new friends, Paine submitted the plans for his bridge to the French Academy of Sciences. By August 29, 1787, his bridge received their official approval, that is, the academy thought it was a worthy scientific invention.

74

The next day Paine left Paris. He crossed the English Channel and went to London. There he used letters from Franklin and Jefferson to meet men with influence. With their help, he submitted his iron bridge to the Royal Society.

There was nothing more Paine could do about building his bridge until he heard from the Royal Society. He left for Thetford to see his parents. But he was too late. His father had died of smallpox on November 14, 1786. His mother was still alive although 90 years old. Paine stayed at the little row house on Bridge Street for three months. Before he left, he arranged to give his mother a pension of nine shillings a week for the remainder of her life. It would well care for her needs in Thetford.

In December 1787, Paine heard that there were plans to build an iron bridge over the Seine River, which runs through the heart of Paris. He rushed back to France. When he tried to sell his bridge plans to the Paris city government, he said he could build it in three months. They asked how he could accomplish such an amazing feat. He proposed to have the iron parts made in the United States and shipped to France. But when the French officials asked the cost, Paine could not tell them exactly how much it would cost. They said no to his proposal. Paine was very disappointed. He needed a bridge contract in Europe because he wanted to return to America and finance the bridge over the Schuykill River himself.

In May 1788, Paine returned to London where several rich men were considering financing the building of his bridge in Britain even without the Royal Society's approval. He met with Peter Whiteside, a rich merchant from Philadelphia. Whiteside offered him a loan. With Whiteside's help, Paine obtained a British patent on the bridge. A patent prevented anyone else from making, using, or selling Paine's invention without his permission. If someone wanted to build an iron bridge, he would have to pay Paine a royalty (money). Paine planned to build a bridge over the Thames River in London. He would make money by charging people a toll to cross it. As he traveled around England looking at ironworks, he interested the large Walker Ironworks in Yorkshire in his idea. They agreed to build, at their own expense, a bridge 210 feet long.

Meanwhile, John Adams, who had been minister (ambassador) to Great Britain, returned to the United States. No new minister was named to take his place, so Paine served as unofficial minister for two years. During this time, he associated with the most highly placed men of England. Any information he learned that was important to the United States he sent to Thomas Jefferson in Paris. These were serious times in Great Britain. King George III had become mentally ill and could not govern.

In France, a whole new government had been formed in June 1789. A National Assembly made up mainly of middle-class people, some clergy, and a few nobles like Lafayette was writing a constitution. They did not intend to get rid of their king as the American colonies had, but they wanted to limit his powers. The king even agreed that some reforms were necessary, but he did not really mean it. The king secretly called out an army of 30,000 men and planned to capture the members of the National Assembly.

When the people of Paris learned of these plans, they were outraged. The king sent his army to march on Paris. The people tried to defend themselves with rocks torn out of the pavement. On July 14, 1789, a crowd of 900, mostly skilled craftsmen who lived nearby, attacked the Bastille, a medieval fortress in Paris used as a prison. They wanted to get gunpowder stored in the fortress. The French people had even fewer rights than the English. For example, men and women could be put in prison for life without a trial. The Bastille represented this injustice. As the crowd battled their way into the Bastille, soldiers began to fire on the crowd, and 98 people were killed. The enraged mob captured the commander of the Bastille, hacked off his head, stuck it on a pike, and carried it around Paris. The king's army was so frightened when they heard the Bastille had fallen that they fled. The next day the mob began tearing down the fortress. The stones were later used to build a bridge over the Seine River. Lafayette acquired the old key to the Bastille. He gave the key as a symbol of revolution to Paine to present to President Washington.

With the fall of the Bastille, mobs rose up all over France. They attacked those who had suppressed them for hundreds of years. The poor peasants burned tax records and documents granting counts and dukes their lands and castles. In the years

On July 14, 1789, a crowd of about 900 attacked the Bastille, a prison that served as a symbol of injustice.

from 1787 through 1789, France had suffered from bad harvests and food shortages. Farmers' incomes fell, but food prices rose. At the same time, economic hardship caused the closing of many textile mills and other industries. Wages were low. Poor people in the towns had to pay three-quarters or even four-fifths of their meager wages just to buy bread.

The National Assembly quickly formed a people's army to keep order and made Lafayette its general. They also passed laws giving the peasants more land and many other privileges long denied them. On August 27, 1789, the National Assembly issued the Declaration of the Rights of Man and of the Citizen written by Lafayette with the help of Jefferson. It stated that all men have civil and humanitarian equal rights. "[M]en are born and remain free and equal in rights . . . liberty, property, security, and resistance to oppression."

When Paine heard this, his revolutionary spirit could resist no longer. He wanted to leave England, return to Paris, and be in the thick of things. But he could not. He was arrested October 29 in London and put into debtors' prison. Peter Whiteside, the merchant who had helped Paine obtain a British patent for his bridge, had gone bankrupt. The men he owed money to learned Paine owed Whiteside a debt of £620, so Paine was arrested, too. He remained in prison three weeks before some friends collected money and got him out. He was freed in November 1789 and left immediately for Paris.

Paine wrote descriptions of all that was going on to his friends in England and the United States. One of them was Edmund Burke, an important member of Parliament from Ireland. Paine had long admired Burke. Burke had supported the repeal of the 1765 Stamp Act with its taxes on newspapers, deeds, and other documents in the colonies. Burke had constantly spoken out for American rights as Englishmen. He and Paine had become good friends while Paine was in England. Paine thought they shared similar opinions on revolution. But in reality they did not, and Paine's letters from France made Burke angry.

On November 1, 1790, Burke published a pamphlet entitled *Reflections on the Revolution in France.* In 356 pages, Burke showed that he did not see anything to admire about the French Revolution. "I do not like to see anything destroyed; any void produced in society; any ruin on the face of the land." He was appalled by the seizure of noble and church lands by the mobs. He called it fraud when the French National Assembly and the people talked of the rights of man. He defended the king and his right to be king as a divine right from God, not a right bestowed by the people. Burke's purpose was to keep peace in his own country and preserve the way its government worked. He severely criticized the Society for Constitutional Information and the Revolution Society (named after the British Revolution of 1688, not the French Revolution) in England. They openly supported the French Revolution. Members of these clubs called for changes in Britain. They demanded the right to vote for all men, annual elections for members of Parliament, and pay for members of Parliament. Some of the more radical members of these and other clubs were accused of wanting to start a revolution in England, too. These were the very societies to which Paine belonged.

In a sentence here and there in *Common Sense* and in the *Crisis* essays, Paine had hinted at encouraging revolution in England. After studying Burke's writing, all the hatred Paine had for the few who ruled the many—and all the ideas and principles he had developed since his childhood in Thetford—spilled out. He wanted the British people to see how bad their government really was. On February 22, 1791, Washington's birthday, he published back in England *Part One* of a pamphlet entitled *The Rights of Man*. Whereas Burke had attacked the French Revolution, Paine vigorously supported it. Much of the pamphlet refuted Burke point for point on the French Revolution. Burke had compared the British Parliament with the French National Assembly saying, *"Fools rush in where angels fear to tread."* Paine answered by saying that the British Parliament is "[l]imited—because not one man in a hundred . . . is admitted to vote." Paine knew this well because his own father had been one of only 31 men in Thetford allowed to vote for members of Parliament.

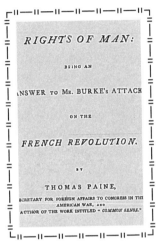

Paine's *The Rights of Man* became a huge best-seller.

Besides refuting Burke, Paine defined government of the people: "[M]en are all of one degree, and consequently . . . all men are born equal, and with equal natural rights." He attacked the idea of being ruled by a monarch. He called absurd the idea of nobles inheriting a right to be lawmaking members of the House of Lords, one of the two houses of Parliament. It was Paine's most brilliant piece of writing; his ideas gave new hope to people. *The Rights of Man* became a best-seller.

Thomas Paine was famous in England. His comings and goings were reported in the newspapers. There was so much demand for his writing that some printers published his old *Crisis* papers. When the British government saw how popular Paine was, they hired a writer named George Chalmers to dig into Paine's first 37 years in England. Under the pen name Francis Oldys, Chalmers wrote about Paine's past as a stay maker. Chalmers blamed Paine for the death of Paine's first wife and his unusual separation from his second. Paine had tried to leave his poor beginnings behind him when he went to America to make a new start. He never spoke of his past. The book affected Paine so strongly that he dropped out of sight for a while.

In the meantime, Paine's 210-foot experimental bridge arrived in London from Yorkshire in May 1791. But he had not raised the money necessary to carry out his plans to span the Thames River with it. Instead, during June and July, he spent long hours every day supervising the construction of his bridge in a field in the village of Paddington near London. For a shilling, people could walk on it as a curiosity. Although the important people were impressed when they came to look at the bridge model, most said it would be too expensive to build the actual bridge. It remained on display for a year. Then it was dismantled and shipped back to Yorkshire. Parts of it were used to build an iron bridge over the River Wear in northern England in 1793. Even though he had a patent, Paine did not receive one penny for the use of his idea. A century later, Paine's design was recognized by engineers as the basis of all arched iron bridges.

For all the success of *The Rights of Man,* Paine was broke again because he gave away copies of his work and his money to further political change and revolution in Britain. He returned to Paris and moved into wretched living quarters because it was all he could afford. When Lafayette found out, he insisted Paine be his guest at his home.

In the meantime, Lafayette himself was in serious trouble. He was in charge of guarding the king and queen. On June 21, 1791, the royal couple tried to escape from their palace in Paris and get across the border into Germany. Lafayette was accused of letting them escape. Four days later, they were caught and returned to Paris. Lafayette was deeply disappointed that the king had been so foolish, for Lafayette wanted to keep the king as part of the new government but with greatly limited royal powers. Paine, however, had been sorry that the royal couple had not made good their escape. He thought a republican government such as that of the United States was the only true government of the people. Paine's

In 1791, the French king and queen were caught trying to flee from France to France's enemy, Germany.

and Lafayette's different ideas caused a split between them. Soon these two great patriots of the American Revolution were no longer friends.

During the time he was a houseguest of Lafayette, Paine had been hard at work on the second part of *The Rights of Man*. He planned to have it printed in London. Then he thought he would go to Ireland and rekindle the Irish revolt against the British.

Paine left Paris in August 1791. By the end of the year, *Part Two* was ready for the printer. But the printers who had published the first part of *The Rights of Man,* J. S. Jordan and Joseph Johnson, rejected Paine's manuscript. They were certain they would be put in prison if their names appeared on it. They finally relented when Paine signed a paper saying he alone was the author and publisher of it. He agreed to take sole responsibility if there was any trouble. *Part Two* of *The Rights of Man* was finally published on February 16, 1792. The first trouble was a joyous one—counting the money. *The Rights of Man* sold more copies than any book ever published in Great Britain up to that time—almost 1.5 million copies.

81

The book was remarkable in that it was so far ahead of its time. Again as in *Common Sense* and the *Crisis* papers, Paine seemed to have a gift for seeing into the future. He suggested many social reforms. Paine said people over 50 should be given a pension by the government. Poor people should be given money to feed themselves and keep a roof over their heads when they could not find work. The government should pay for poor children to be educated in "reading, writing, and common arithmetic . . . ignorance will be banished from the rising generation, and the number of poor will hereafter become less, because their abilities, by the aid of education, will be greater." He even said that the homeless (he had once been homeless himself) should be housed and helped to find work at government expense. Soldiers and sailors should receive a pension for life. Workmen should not have to work for wages fixed by the government and not changed for years. Here he gave a history of the plight of the excise tax men. He spoke out against parents' money going to their eldest son, a practice that left their other children penniless. Perhaps he was thinking of how his mother had not inherited any money from her well-to-do family and had had to marry a poor stay maker. He even gave a detailed study of the British national budget and how it could be changed to pay for these programs.

If Paine had stuck to reforms, he would have been all right. In fact, Prime Minister William Pitt introduced a law in Parliament to give soldiers and sailors pensions. But the success of *Part One* of *The Rights of Man* had really gone to his head when he made the statement: "I published the Pamphlet 'Common Sense.' The success it met with was beyond anything since the invention of printing." He now openly called for revolution. "From a small spark kindled in America, a flame had arisen not to be extinguished." He went on to say, "If universal peace, civilization, and commerce, are ever to be the happy lot of man, it cannot be accomplished but by a revolution in the system of governments."

The British government did not want to let these ideas loose among the people because they would stir up trouble. Even Gouverneur Morris, appointed U.S. minister to France in early 1792 to replace Jefferson, said that Paine had gone too far and would be punished. Why did Paine place himself at such risk? He wrote, "Independence is my happiness, and I view things as they are, without regard to place or person; my country is the world, and my religion is to do good."

The British government did not really want to arrest him. That would make him a hero. Instead, they began a program of harassment, hoping Paine would go back to France and leave England alone. The government arrested Jordan, the publisher of *The Rights of Man.* Frightened by the thought of a prison term, he promptly pleaded guilty to printing seditious works and paid a fine—much to Paine's disgust. The government hired mobs to attack people who supported the French Revolution. They also hung and burned a dummy representing Paine in several cities. Thomas Paine was arrested—not for what he had written—but on a false debt charge. He was quickly released.

This 1791 anti-Paine cartoon made fun of him by calling him "Mad Tom."

On May 21, 1792, the government informed Paine he would be put on trial. The charge was seditious libel, which meant writing to encourage violent or illegal changes in the government or rebellion against the government. Prime Minister Pitt also persuaded King George III to issue a royal proclamation against all writers, printers, and sellers of seditious writing. But the proclamation had the reverse effect. People bought more copies than ever of *The Rights of Man.* Paine said, "It is a dangerous attempt in any government to say to a nation, '*thou shalt not read.'"* Paine clearly had the whole British government worried. He twitted them by writing, "Ye silly swains, thought I to myself, why do you torment yourselves thus? The 'Rights of Man' is a book calmly and rationally written; why then are you so disturbed?" They were disturbed because they had seen what his writing of *Common Sense* had cost them in America. They saw Paine as not just an annoying troublemaker but a dangerous man. In June, the government postponed Paine's trial until December 18 in order to have time to build a stronger case against him.

In early September, a committee of French gentlemen arrived to see Paine. They pleaded with him to return with them. He had been made an honorary citizen of France along with Washington and others for their sympathy with the French revolutionary cause. What is more, Paine had been chosen by the people of the Calais district of France to represent them in the new lawmaking body, the National Convention, which was to begin meeting in late September. Paine decided to accept.

Paine and his friends thought it best to leave England as quietly as possible. At Dover, where Paine had once worked as a stay maker, they boarded the boat to cross the English Channel to Calais.

Even though glad to be rid of Paine, the British government put him on trial *in absentia*—without his being present—as scheduled December 18. Although the most successful lawyer in England, Sir John Erskine, defended him, Paine sealed his own guilty verdict. He had left behind in England a letter denouncing the suppression of his writing and criticizing the whole government from top to bottom. He wrote a letter to Sir Archibald MacDonald, who was the prosecutor for the government in the case against him. In it, Paine explained why he could not be there to defend himself. "The duty I am now engaged in is of too much importance to permit me to trouble myself about your prosecution." He gave a final blast at the British government. He claimed that "the Government of England is as great, if not the greatest, perfection of fraud and corruption that ever took place since governments began." Paine was as rebellious as ever. As a result of this trial, he was declared outlawed from Great Britain forever.

CHAPTER EIGHT

Citizen Paine

Thomas Paine left England a fugitive from a criminal trial and—if he were found guilty—from prison. When Paine reached France, he was given a hero's welcome. A salute by the cannons of a nearby fortress announced the arrival of his boat. Crowds shouted "Vive Thomas Paine" for hours. Parades and speeches in his honor went on for three days. During his journey to Paris, towns along the way gave parties in his honor. When Paine reached Paris on September 19, 1792, he went to the National Convention. As he entered the hall, the delegates stood and cheered him because Paine's writings had helped support the French Revolution.

But the French Revolution had changed while Paine had been in England. In April 1792, France had declared war on Bohemia (now part of the Czech Republic), Hungary, Prussia (now part of Germany and Poland), and Austria. The French hoped to spread the revolution throughout Europe. But Prussia was a strong military power and soon turned the tables by invading France. Frightened people from the French countryside flooded into Paris ahead of the Prussians. The people of Paris had not been in favor of starting the war until their needs for food and basic rights had been met. Now they lost all faith in the French government. On August 10, 1792, they revolted, led by shopkeepers and tradesmen and joined by poor workers and by ruffians and criminals from the streets of Paris. These radicals called themselves *sans-culottes* (people who

Sans-culottes

85

In August 1792, mobs of sans-culottes attack the royal palace and stab, stone, and club to death more than 600 of the guards.

didn't wear trousers that stopped at the knee, as the aristocrats did, but wore long pants instead). Thousands marched to the city hall of Paris where they seized the mayor and put him under arrest. They pushed on to the king's palace and battled his guards, killing most of them. The mob forced the frightened Legislative Assembly to arrest the king. Then they made the Legislative Assembly call new elections for members to a National Convention to write a new constitution.

In September 1792, the leaders of the sans-culottes ordered the arrests of hundreds of nobles, priests, and others, who they thought did not support the Revolution. Then the mob went mad and in three days massacred 1,300 of these helpless prisoners in unspeakably barbaric ways. A princess who had been arrested had her arms and legs torn off and fired from cannons. Many prisoners were beheaded. This September Massacre ended only two weeks before Paine landed at Calais.

The first official session of the new National Convention was September 21. Paine was 1 of only 2 foreigners out of 749 delegates. The other was a Prussian known as Anacharsis Cloots. Paine thought this revolution was going to be like the American Revolution. With his experience he would lead the way. Being 20 to 30 years older than the young French leaders, he saw himself as another Benjamin Franklin, the elder statesman. But the political, economic, and social conditions were entirely different in France from what they had been in the American colonies. The delegates to the National Convention began fighting each other for power. One group was called the Girondists. They wanted to follow the example of the United States' revolution. The others were the more radical Jacobins. A third and largest group were some 500 members who were not committed to either party.

One of the first laws passed was to declare France a republic. The delegates abolished the titles of the king and all royalty and nobility—no more dukes, lords, and counts. Not even any more courtesy titles like madame, monsieur, or mademoiselle. Everyone hereafter would be addressed as "citizen." France abolished the use of the world calendar for itself. Instead of 1792, the year would henceforth be Year One. Paine saw a second country rid itself of a monarchy, and he was delighted.

Now that France was a republic, what were the French going to do with their former king? Differing opinions divided the delegates. The radical Jacobins wanted him brought to trial; the more moderate Girondists did not. The Girondists tried to save Louis XVI from trial by calling for a vote among all the people of France on what should happen to him. His old enemy, England—wanting to stop the killing of kings before the trend reached its shores—even tried to save him by threatening war if he was brought to trial. But in November, secret papers were discovered. They showed that King Louis XVI had conspired with foreign governments to help him put down the Revolution. On December 11, 1792, the trial of King Louis XVI on charges of treason began. It must have given Paine a strange feeling to know he himself was also on trial in England at the same time.

The king was found guilty. Although many of his French friends were Girondists, Thomas Paine considered himself above any party, neither a Girondist or Jacobin. On January 15, 1793, Paine spoke to the National Convention pleading for the king's life to be spared. "Citizen President: My hatred and abhorrence of monarchy are sufficiently known." But he said he was indebted to this king, Louis, for "[i]t is to France alone, I know, that the United States of America owe that support which enabled them to shake off the unjust and tyrannical yoke of Britain." Then he proposed a plan to let Louis and his family leave France. "Let then those United States be the safeguard and asylum [a place safe from arrest] of Louis Capet. . . . [I]n submitting this proposition, I consider myself as a citizen of both countries. I submit it as a citizen of America, who feels the debt of gratitude which he owes to every Frenchman."

On January 16 and 17, the delegates voted on what the king's punishment would be. Each voted for Louis's death until Paine's name was called. In French, he said he voted for banishment to the United States. This gave other delegates the courage to vote for banishment, too. But the final tally was for death. On January 19, Paine made yet another plea to save Louis's life. It was read in French for him by another member. (Paine did not speak or write French well.) Only the first sentence had been spoken when Jean-Paul Marat, a leader of the Jacobins, interrupted. He said Paine had no right to vote on the death penalty because he was a Quaker who was against capital punishment. Marat was shouted down, and Paine's speech continued. He said the United States was France's only ally and would be very sorry to see Louis put to death. This was really a threat. Marat interrupted again saying the French translator was not reading the words of Thomas Paine. Paine, standing beside the translator, insisted those were his words.

Marat was a doctor and journalist. But when the French Revolution had begun, he became a radical, popular among the poor workers of Paris. In violent speeches, Marat accused his political opponents of being traitors. He dressed as a ragged sans-culotte and wore a pistol in his belt. He had sunken wild eyes and a terrible skin disease that made him appear fearsome. He was thought to be responsible for inciting the mobs to commit the terrible acts of the September Massacre. No one wanted him for an enemy.

The day after Paine's speech and his row with Marat, the Convention announced its final decision—the king was to be put to death. Louis was guillotined on January 21, 1793.

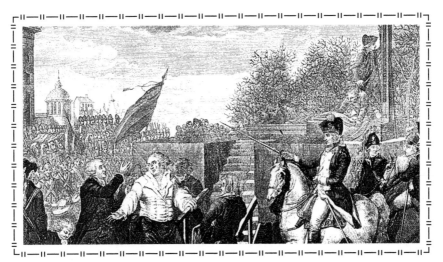

Louis XVI about to have his head chopped off. Paine made enemies among French radicals because he opposed the execution.

On February 1, France declared war on Britain, Holland, and
Spain. The French hoped that this would encourage the British
and Dutch poor to rise up in revolution. However, they did not.
The French army suffered a serious defeat in Belgium because
military supplies were withheld by the Jacobins to discredit the
Girondists. French General Charles Dumouriez saw how corrupt
the Revolution had become. He deserted to the Austrians and
joined Lafayette already in an Austrian prison. Lafayette had
opposed the Jacobins and had then been declared a traitor by the
Legislative Assembly. In August 1792, believing there was nothing
more he could do to help his country, Lafayette had fled to Belgium.
There, the Austrians, who controlled Belgium, imprisoned him,
despite his protests that he was an American general.

There were more troubles. The National Convention passed a
draft law, which forced men to serve in the army. The law caused
uprisings in several parts of the country. Inflation had made French
money almost worthless. Food shortages and unemployment persist-
ed. On April 6, 1793, the National Convention appointed nine members to a Committee of Public Safety with broad legal powers to deal
with these problems. The committee carried out radical measures to
supply the army with weapons and the poor with bread.

At the same time, Marat issued a public letter saying there was a counterrevolution going on in the National Convention. He called the National Convention a "nest of traitors." The Convention put Marat on trial for these statements, saying they could lead to anarchy and a return of the massacres. Paine had never forgiven Marat for interrupting his speech in January. If he had not, the king's life might have been saved. Paine testified at the trial that Marat had once told him republicanism was only a fantastic dream. Marat's statement could have been considered antirevolutionary. It did not work. Marat went free. The outcome of the trial made Marat stronger than ever. (A few months later, Marat was assassinated and became an instant martyred hero.)

Marat's trial made the more radical sans-culottes even bolder. They insisted that the National Convention expel 22 members they did not like. All were Girondists. Fortunately, Paine's name was not on that list. The Convention at first refused to expel the 22 members. Instead, the Convention arrested several leaders of the sans-culottes.

On May 31, early in the morning, the sans-culottes sealed off the city from the rest of the country. About 80,000 of them marched on the National Convention to present more demands. The Convention rejected them. The sans-culottes ordered the National Guard to arrest the Girondist leaders and not to allow any delegate in or out. When Paine tried to enter, he was stopped. A friend told him to get away or he might be put on the list to be arrested, too. Inside the Convention, the delegates voted to march out together through the mob and soldiers. But when they saw the soldiers' guns aimed at them, they returned to their seats and passed every law the sans-culottes wanted. A total of 29 delegates were expelled and arrested. Almost 100 others quit the Convention in disgust.

With all the strife going on in Paris, Paine moved his living quarters to the quiet suburb of St. Denis. He no longer attended the Convention. He had given up on the Revolution he had had such high hopes for less than a year before. He now believed that the French Revolution had turned into an opportunity for some men to use the mobs to grab power for themselves. The rights of man were ground into the dust. Paine began writing a book on his religious beliefs. He planned to entitle it *The Age of Reason.*

In July 1793, Maximilien Robespierre, who had been a fellow delegate with Paine from Calais, had been named to the Committee of Public Safety. From then on, one by one, Paine had seen his Girondist friends arrested. When all the Girondists were gone from the National Convention and the Jacobins had control of it, they passed a Law of Suspects in September. Anyone— noble, priest, peasant, man, woman, or even child—could be arrested, put through a brief mockery of a trial, and executed. Marie-Antoinette, the queen of France, was executed in October. Then the Girondists, among them Paine's friends, were guillotined by order of the Committee of Public Safety. The purpose of this Reign of Terror was to get rid of any opposition. Over the next year, thousands of people in Paris were killed. Almost 250,000 people were slaughtered in other parts of France; hundreds of thousands of people were imprisoned.

Paine was determined to leave France. But he could not. France and Britain were at war. If Paine's ship were seized by the British, he could be put in prison or hanged because he was an outlaw. Besides, the French would not let him leave. He had been officially declared a traitor to the Revolution simply because he was an Englishman. On December 25, the National Convention passed a decree that no foreigner could represent the French people. They did not mention Paine or Cloots by name. Paine, too late, realized he had been marked as an "enemy of the nation" from the day he had defended King Louis. The soldiers came for Thomas Paine at three o'clock in the morning of December 28, 1793, and took him off to prison.

Girondists being taken to their execution.

91

Prison

Thomas Paine and Anacharsis Cloots, the two foreign members of the National Convention, were taken to the Luxembourg Prison together. The prison had once been a palace, so Paine was not thrown into a dungeon. He was given a room on the ground floor looking out on the garden. Three Frenchmen shared the room with him. Prisoners were free to roam about the prison during the day. There were many people for him to talk to. Among those in the prison were Englishmen and women like himself whose only crime was that they were foreigners. Paine was not particularly concerned. The reason was that other Americans who had been taken to Luxembourg had been released within weeks. Surely, he thought, as an important American he would be released even sooner.

Sixteen Americans got up a petition for Paine's release and marched to the National Convention to present it. They claimed Paine as an American and promised he would leave the country as soon as possible. But the president of the Convention rejected their petition. He claimed that Paine had to be considered an Englishman because he was born in England. Therefore, he was the citizen of an enemy country.

When that failed, Paine had no choice but to appeal to Gouverneur Morris, the U.S. minister to France. Years earlier, Morris had sided against Paine in the Silas Deane affair. Morris advised Paine to lay low and try not to be noticed. Angrily, Paine refused to do nothing and remain in prison for he knew not how long. He pestered Morris until finally Morris wrote a short letter to the French foreign minister on Paine's behalf. But he did not demand Paine's release as an American citizen. Morris did nothing more to help him. President Washington's official policy was that if United States citizens broke the laws of foreign countries, they could expect punishment. Washington did not help

Lafayette, a prisoner in Austria, either. He did not believe the United States presidency should be used to intervene in such matters.

The United States had changed since Paine had left. The Articles of Confederation had been abandoned. A new Constitution had been drawn up in Philadelphia during the long, hot summer of 1787. It gave more power to the President and to Congress, less to the states. George Washington had been elected as the first President in early 1789.

Two factions that soon became political parties had developed in the United States. The Federalists led by Washington wanted better relations with Great Britain. The anti-Federalists under Jefferson wanted better relations with France. Paine suspected that he had been put in prison so he could not go back to the United States or even write to the United States. The French feared that he might tell damaging facts about the French Revolution. As a member of the National Convention, he knew too much. Maximilien Robespierre considered journalists dangerous to the cause of the French Revolution, and Paine the most dangerous of all.

Diplomatic relations between France and the United States had become troubled in 1793. President Washington insisted the United States remain neutral in France's war with Great Britain. France thought the United States should keep its promises made in the 1778 Treaty of Alliance and fight on France's side. In July, Washington had insulted France by asking that its ambassador to the United States be withdrawn. The French ambassador had been insisting on resupplying French warships in American ports. This made the French revolutionaries very angry at the United States and all Americans.

Another problem for Paine was that his friend Jefferson had resigned as U.S. secretary of state on January 5, 1794. He could not have heard of Paine's plight until long after he retired to his home in Virginia. Even then, he had little power to help him.

In March, all communications between people inside and outside the prison was cut off. That same month, Cloots was guillotined. Paine wrote later, "The state of things in the prisons was a continued scene of horror. No man could count upon life for

93

twenty-four hours. . . . Scarcely a night passed in which ten, twenty, thirty, forty, fifty, or more were not taken out of the prison, carried before a pretended tribunal in the morning and guillotined before night." One day, Thomas Paine was marked for execution.

> The room in which I was lodged was on the ground floor, and one of a long range of rooms under a gallery, and the door of it opened outward and flat against the wall; so that when it was open the inside of the door appeared outward, and the contrary when it was shut. . . . When persons by scores and by hundreds were to be taken out of the prison for the guillotine it was always done in the night, and those who performed that office had a private mark or signal, by which they knew what rooms to go to, and what number to take. We, as I have stated, were four, and the door of our room was marked, unobserved by us, with that number in chalk; but it happened, if happening is a proper word, that the mark was put on when the door was open, and flat against the wall, and thereby came on the inside when we shut it at night, and the destroying angel passed by it.

It was a narrow escape.

Going to bed every night in a candleless room not knowing if he would still be alive the next night was too much of a strain for the 57-year-old Paine. He became so ill with a fever that he was out of his head for almost a month. Two English doctors, also prisoners, cared for him or he never would have pulled through. When he recovered, he learned that in July the National Convention had seized Robespierre and executed him. The Reign of Terror was over, and the prisons began to empty.

Paine was not released, but he could communicate with the outside world again. He began bombarding the French government with letters. Then in August he learned that Gouverneur Morris had been replaced as U.S. minister to France by Paine's good friend James Monroe. Paine immediately wrote letters to

94

Prisoners react to the calling out of the names of people to be executed. Paine was also imprisoned and barely escaped death.

Monroe impressing upon him that he lived in constant danger of execution. Although the Reign of Terror had lifted, Paine greatly feared that it could return at any time on any excuse. At last, Monroe managed to free Paine on November 4, 1794. He was so shocked at Paine's frail health that he invited him to stay at his house until he regained his strength.

The last thing Paine had done before he was imprisoned was to slip the manuscript for *The Age of Reason* to a friend. While he was cut off from the outside world, it was printed in France, England, and America. Paine said he had always intended to write his views on religion at the end of his life. Knowing he faced prison, he had reason to think the end of his life might be very near. The other reason he wrote it was that the leaders of the French Revolution were trying to de-Christianize the country. The 700-year-old Notre Dame Cathedral in Paris had already been changed into the secular Temple of Reason. Paine saw

France headed toward atheism, the belief that there is no God. He offered the French people deism instead. Deism was a 17th- and 18th-century movement whose followers believed in religion based on human reason and morality. They believed in one God who created the world and the laws governing it. Deists believed that after that God did not interfere in those laws. Paine wrote, "The only idea man can affix to the name of God is that of a first cause, the cause of all things." Deism was part of the Age of Enlightenment, the use of reason to question everything. "Every science has for its basis a system of principles as fixed and unalterable as those by which the universe is regulated and governed. Man cannot make principles, he can only discover them," Paine wrote. A number of men of science and learning in the 17th and 18th centuries were deists including Washington, Jefferson, and Franklin. But they were quiet about it. Many people considered deism to be blasphemy—showing great disrespect for God and disagreeing with religious doctrines.

Paine explained his personal beliefs:

> I believe in one God, and no more; and I hope for happiness beyond this life.
>
> I believe in the equality of man; and I believe that religious duties consist in doing justice, loving mercy, and endeavoring to make our fellow-creatures happy.
>
> But, lest it should be supposed that I believe many other things in addition to these, I shall, in the progress of this work, declare the things I do not believe, and my reasons for not believing them.
>
> I do not believe in the creed professed by the Jewish Church, by the Roman Church, by the Greek Church, by the Turkish Church, by the Protestant Church, nor by any church that I know of. My own mind is my own church.

At the end of *The Age of Reason*, Paine wrote, "[L]et every man follow, as he has a right to do, the religion and the worship he prefers."

Much of *The Age of Reason* discussed the universe as proof of the existence of God. Paine gave a detailed and very accurate description of the earth's solar system and how it worked. He had learned this as a young man when he had purchased his globes and orrery and talked to Dr. John Bevis, James Ferguson, and Benjamin Martin.

In France, government leaders just shrugged their shoulders. The Frenchman Voltaire had already expressed his ideas about deism 50 years earlier. Besides, they believed that Paine's arguments against Christianity helped spread atheism, which was what the French government wanted.

In England, it was a different matter. Paine's friends and supporters were shocked by what he had written, and many turned away from him. The British government severely persecuted anyone who had anything to do with *The Age of Reason*. A printer of *The Age of Reason* was convicted of blasphemy and sent to prison for a year. Reading it was a serious crime, which could result in being sent to Australia and the prison colonies there. Spies reported about those who even discussed it. The Church of England was a state-supported church. Some leaders considered ideas opposed to the established church to be as dangerous to those in power as revolutionary ideas.

When *Part One* of *The Age of Reason* appeared in the United States, the reaction was milder than that in Britain. The First Amendment, added to the U.S. Constitution in 1791, protected freedom of religion. It also prevented the national government from establishing a government-supported religion.

But in the United States *Part Two* of *The Age of Reason* caused a firestorm. To answer his critics, in 1795 Paine had written *Part Two* of *The Age of Reason,* in which he went through the Bible book by book and tried to discredit it. Many Americans had braved all the dangers of coming to the New World so they could practice their own deeply held religious beliefs. Many people were horrified at what Paine had written. The only excuse they could find was that he had gone mad in prison.

It is true that Paine had undergone severe mental and physical stress the 10 months he was in prison. He felt he had been abandoned by the United States, and he was consumed by bitterness especially against President George Washington.

Monroe persuaded Paine not to send several caustic letters he had written to Washington. But Paine had to get his revenge. In 1796, he smuggled to the United States an open letter to Washington. It included the letters he had previously written, the ones Monroe had stopped him from sending. The open letter was printed by Franklin's grandson, Benjamin Franklin Bache, who hated Washington. (Benjamin Franklin had died in 1790.)

Paine stated in this letter, "I do not hesitate to say that you have not served America with more disinterestedness, or greater zeal, or more fidelity, than myself. . . . It is time, Sir, to speak the undisguised language of historical truth." Of the Battle of Boston in 1776, Paine said, "The commencement [beginning] of his (Washington's) command was the commencement of inactivity. Nothing was afterwards done, or attempted to be done, during the nine months he remained before Boston." Paine made no mention of Washington's brilliant maneuver on Dorchester Heights, which had driven the British out of Boston. Paine said the evacuation of Fort Lee, in which he had taken part, was successful owing to General Greene. He never mentioned that it was General Washington who rode into the fort and directed the evacuation himself. Paine's claims in this open letter contradicted his own words written 15 years earlier in the *Crisis* papers. He even went so far as to accuse George Washington of being in league with Robespierre to keep him in prison.

In the final paragraph, Paine leveled his worst blast:

> And as to you, Sir, treacherous in private friendship (for so you have been to me, and that in the day of danger) and a hypocrite in public life, the world will be puzzled to decide whether you are an apostate or an impostor; whether you have abandoned good principles, or whether you ever had any.

As a result of this open letter, Monroe asked Paine to leave his house where Paine had been living for a year and a half. President Washington did not dignify such unfair charges with a public answer. The newspapers called Paine "Mad Tom." William Cobbett, an English journalist and writer, republished Francis

Oldys's dreadful biography of Paine's early life in England with all its falsehoods. Vicious slanders and outrageous lies were printed in newspapers or passed by word of mouth about Paine. But people were ready to believe them. Paine became one of the most hated men of his time. His reputation, even a century later, was still seriously injured by his letter to Washington and *The Age of Reason.*

In 1795, the National Convention had voted to restore Paine and 73 other delegates it had expelled during the Reign of Terror. The delegates were in the process of writing yet another constitution. On July 7, Paine made a speech reminding them of the rights of man and the original principles of the French Revolution. His main objection to the new constitution was that not every man could vote. Only soldiers and those who owned a certain amount of property could. Paine wrote the following:

> The true and only true basis of representative government is equality of rights. Every man has a right to one vote, and no more in the choice of representatives. The rich have no more right to exclude the poor from the right of voting, or of electing and being elected, than the poor have to exclude the rich.

But the delegates did not listen to him. Under the new constitution, France was governed by an Assembly made up of two houses of representatives to make laws but elected by only 30,000 Frenchmen. Paine was not elected as one of the representatives; he was out of a job again. The Assembly appointed five men as Directors to run the country. But in the elections of 1797 the people voted out most of the representatives. In their place, the voters had chosen representatives who wanted a constitutional monarchy—a government in which a king would have limited powers. But three of the five Directors wanted to keep France a republic. These Directors ordered 12,000 troops to Paris. Those in the Assembly who did not agree with the republican Directors were forced out. The Directors began to govern as dictators supported by the army. The French people were almost back where they had started eight years before—no representation, ongoing wars, and not enough bread. Thomas Paine decided to go home.

James Monroe had been recalled as minister to France by John Adams, the new President. Paine wanted to go with him. But Monroe did not want to return to the United States with the hated Paine as a traveling companion. Paine was persuaded to take another ship from another port. He went to Le Havre and stayed three or four months waiting for an American ship. Then he heard that Monroe's ship had been stopped and searched in the middle of the Atlantic Ocean by the British, who were looking for Paine. He decided to return to Paris instead of sailing to the United States.

Paine was invited to live with the family of Nicolas de Bonneville, a revolutionary printer and publisher. De Bonneville often printed articles by Paine in his newspaper *Le Bien Informé*, "The Informed Good." One of these articles described a scheme Paine had come up with to use small gunboats to invade England. He even sent money to the French government to get the project started. One day the national hero of France, General Napoleon Bonaparte, called at the de Bonneville home to discuss Paine's plan with him. The best place to invade, Paine told him, was the deserted beach along the North Sea at Alford; he knew it well. Napoleon asked Paine to accompany him as his political adviser when he launched the invasion of England. He even went so far as to order the gunboats to be built. Then Napoleon was sent to fight in Egypt and Paine's plan was forgotten.

In 1798, another election to the two houses of the Assembly was held. A majority was won by men who wanted another new constitution and a return of more radical Jacobin government. The Directors in 1797 had opposed those who wanted a king; now they opposed the radicals. The Directors forced 106 of the representatives to resign by falsely charging that they wanted to revive the Reign of Terror. Paine kept quiet this time. The Directors still used the guillotine, and several of his friends who had spoken out had lost their heads.

In Egypt, Napoleon was severely defeated by the British admiral, Lord Horatio Nelson, in the Battle of the Nile on August 1, 1798. The French fleet was destroyed. Napoleon's army was blockaded by the British fleet and unable to escape from Egypt.

After Napoleon seized power, Paine's hopes for a free, republican France faded and he decided to return to the United States.

Napoleon got away by crossing the Mediterranean Sea in a small boat and returning to France. With the backing of the army in France, he seized power on November 9, 1799. The army forced the National Assembly to disband at the point of bayonets. Napoleon set up a new government of three men he called the Consulate. He appointed himself First Consul with a term of office of 10 years. In reality, Napoleon had become the dictator of France. This ended the French Revolution.

101

When Paine's friend Thomas Jefferson was elected President in 1800. Paine wrote to him saying he longed to return to America. But he still feared the British would capture him on the high seas. Jefferson replied that an American warship, the *Maryland,* was coming to France and Paine was welcome to return on it. Paine was so proud of this letter, he published it to show how important he was to an American president. This brought torrents of criticism down on Jefferson. The Federalist press accused him of sending a warship to France just to pick up the hated Paine. Quickly, Jefferson issued a denial. He said the ship was going for other reasons. What he had offered Paine was no more than he would offer any other American citizen. He reminded the country of Paine's past services during the American Revolution. Paine saw that it was better to decline Jefferson's offer and stay in France.

In March 1802, France and Britain finally signed a truce in their war. At last it was safe for Paine to cross the Atlantic back to the United States. He set sail on September 2, 1802, from Le Havre where he had landed 15 years before.

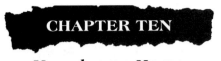
Unwelcome Home

Paine's ship tied up at Baltimore on October 30, 1802, after a 60-day crossing. Much to his surprise, a welcoming party of anti-Federalists was on the dock to meet him. They carried him off to a nearby tavern for a dinner to celebrate his return. Paine thought this was a good beginning. He was 65 years old, an age when most men had long since retired from their business. Not Paine. He was full of plans and high hopes. With him he carried new bridge models he had worked on in France with Robert Fulton, the famous American inventor. He hoped that President Thomas Jefferson would persuade Congress to give money to build these bridges all over the country.

Within the week, Paine left Baltimore for the new capital city in the District of Columbia. He was disgusted that it was called Washington. Paine called it Federal City. When he tried to find a room at a hotel, he was really struck by what people thought of him. Several innkeepers refused to have him because their other guests threatened to leave if Paine stayed. He finally found rooms at Lovett's Hotel under an assumed name.

Despite others' opinions, President Thomas Jefferson invited Paine to the White House often. Jefferson liked Paine and thought the country owed him a great debt; certainly it owed him honor, at least. Jefferson was not shocked by *The Age of Reason*. He agreed with the principles of deism. But his open friendship for Paine caused outrage among a majority of Americans and made them suspicious of Jefferson.

In the weeks after his return, the newspapers in all the states ran stories about him. The newspapers of the Federalists were hateful; the anti-Federalists recalled his past glories. The stories in the newspapers at first amused him. But when they threatened Jefferson, Paine had to answer them. Within two weeks of returning to America, he published a public letter entitled *To the*

When Paine returned to the United States, he was met with either indifference or hatred. Many disliked his book *The Age of Reason*.

Citizens of the United States. He told the American people what he had been doing for 15 years. He also warned them that the Federalists were trying to take away their liberty.

A second Paine letter, a week later, again attacked the Federalists and singled out former President John Adams. Paine objected to John Adams's idea of a republic as a country of laws and not of men. Paine asked, What if the laws were bad? He accused John Adams of wanting to be the king and his sons kings after him.

This was followed by a third letter charging that the Federalists had tried to start a war between France and the United States during the 1790s. He described his imprisonment in France and his near miss with the guillotine. Paine revived his charges against Washington, although Washington had been dead three years. He said there had been a reign of terror in the United States at the end of the Washington administration and during Adams's presidency. This, of course, was untrue. However, during the late 1790s, there had been a growing conflict between the Federalists and the anti-Federalists. Fear of the violence of the French Revolution and hostility to foreigners led Congress to pass the Alien and Sedition Acts of 1798. These laws limited freedom of speech, freedom of the press, and the rights of foreigners living in the United States.

Paine was going too far in his accusations even for the anti-Federalists. He was hurting Jefferson more than helping him. But President Jefferson stood firmly behind Paine to let him write as he pleased because Jefferson thought he had a good heart.

President Jefferson wanted Paine's advice on matters of government. As soon as the American Revolution had ended, American settlers moved west across the Appalachian Mountains. They settled on land as far as the Mississippi River, the western border of the United States. The settlers shipped the products they grew or made to New Orleans by way of the network of rivers flowing into the Mississippi. In the city of New Orleans, a port well situated on the Mississippi River near the Gulf of Mexico, they sold these products. Spain, which controlled New Orleans, kept the port open to American goods. In 1801, Napoleon wanted New Orleans as a base to build an empire in

North America. Spain a weak country, agreed to give it to France and closed the port to American goods. The western settlers threatened to seize New Orleans by force to keep it open. But President Jefferson offered to buy New Orleans and part of northern Florida from France. When Jefferson consulted Paine on the idea, Paine told him France's treasury was empty and Napoleon would welcome the money. Instead of just selling New Orleans and part of Florida, Napoleon offered the United States all of what was then called Louisiana. This was a huge area much larger than today's state of Louisiana. It included land from the Gulf of Mexico to Canada and from the Mississippi River to the Rocky Mountains. James Monroe and Robert R. Livingston, whom Jefferson had appointed to work out the purchase, thought this was a bargain. They agreed to pay $15 million for it. France was, indeed, willing to sell it for that amount.

The Federalists were outraged. Jefferson had avoided war by buying Louisiana. They wanted all-out war with France. In the first place, they argued, Congress had only authorized $2 million to buy New Orleans. To pay $15 million meant the United States would have to go into debt by borrowing large sums from foreign bankers in England and Holland. They pointed out there was nothing in the Constitution about purchasing land. The debate raged on during most of 1803. Paine's pen scribbled public essays in support of the Louisiana Purchase. His private letters to Jefferson were full of advice.

Meanwhile, Paine sent a long letter to Congress about his iron bridge. But Jefferson thought the states, not the federal government, should build their own bridges. Paine had hoped for a government job to support himself, but Jefferson did not offer him one. Although Jefferson liked Paine, everyone recognized he was unpredictable and often drank too much. Jefferson remembered the Silas Deane affair in 1777 when Paine had made government secrets public. Paine also caused trouble when he published Jefferson's personal letter offering the passage on the *Maryland* to come home from Europe. In February 1803, Paine left Washington taking his bridge models with him.

He stopped in Philadelphia to see old friends. Some welcomed him. Others like Benjamin Rush refused to speak to him because of *The Age of Reason.* His iron bridge model was put on display in Independence Hall.

Paine did not tarry long. He had to get to Bordentown. When he arrived at his friend Colonel Joseph Kirkbride's house, he found Madame de Bonneville and her three young sons waiting for him. Paine had lived with Nicolas de Bonneville and his family for five years. When the French government shut down de Bonneville's presses, Paine urged the family to go to America. The French government would not let Nicolas leave. However, his wife and sons were free to go. Paine promised to be responsible for them. The family landed in Newport, Virginia, a few weeks after Paine arrived in Baltimore in late 1802. Following Paine's instructions, Madame de Bonneville, unable to speak the language, nevertheless had made her way to Bordentown.

Paine left the family at the home of the generous Kirkbrides and went on to New York City. He had much advice and letters of introduction to important people who could help James Monroe, one of America's leaders talking to French officials about the purchase of Louisiana.

On his way, Paine had another unpleasant taste of how some of the American public hated him. Colonel Kirkbride had driven him to nearby Trenton to catch a stagecoach to New York. But the stage driver refused to take Paine. When Kirkbride and Paine tried to drive their carriage away, a jeering crowd gathered and made noise to frighten their horses.

In New York, Paine's reception was very different. He was given a big banquet on March 18 by the anti-Federalists. On July 4, he was guest of honor at a celebration in New York where he read some of his poetry.

In the meantime, Congress finally ratified the treaty to purchase Louisiana in October. The United States took possession of it on December 20, 1803, doubling the size of the country. Paine could take pride in the fact that he was one of the first to suggest that the United States purchase all of the huge territory, not just New Orleans.

But Paine had to think about making money to support himself since none of his plans had worked out. He returned to his farm in New Rochelle in New York State to cut wood and sell it for winter fuel in New York City. His house and barn had burned down in 1793, but a small cottage remained. Soon after he arrived in New Rochelle he fell ill again and was partially paralyzed.

By January 1804, Paine had recovered enough to return to New York City where he was surprised to see Madame de Bonneville and her children. She told Paine she refused to live in rural Bordentown another day. But unfortunately she had no money to live in New York. Paine had to pay her bills, which were considerable. Madame did not know the meaning of the word *thrift* in either English or French. Paine set her up in business as a teacher of the French language.

He returned to his New Rochelle farm in the spring of 1804. That was where he was going to have to make his home from now on. His friend Colonel Kirkbride, with whom he often had lived, had died in November 1803.

Paine had a large farm with good land, oxen, a horse, a cow, pigs, and farm tools. But soon after his return, his tenant farmer quit. Paine knew nothing about farming, or he forgot what his father had taught him when he helped him work their few acres in Thetford. He could not find another tenant, so the farm produced no income for him. Paine thought he might live as long as his parents so he had to conserve his money. He ate little—bread, fruit, and milk from his cow, but he seldom purchased meat. A visitor reported he even dried his tea leaves so he could reuse them. His health had not been good since he had been in prison. This poor diet only made him weaker. He finally sold off some land for $4,000. With the money, he made plans to expand his house and build a workshop. But all Paine really wanted to do was write.

A steady stream of letters went to newspapers and to Jefferson, Madison, Monroe, and George Clinton, now governor of New York State and later vice president of the United States. Paine was delighted when Jefferson won reelection in 1804 over the Federalists, who were still trying to use Paine to discredit him.

In 1805, Paine offered to return to France. He thought he could help Monroe by giving him the benefit of his experience with Napoleon. Napoleon had started up another war by attack-

Paine did not spend much time at his New Rochelle farm. He did
stay for a while in this house in Greenwich Village in Manhattan.

ing Austria. Jefferson wrote thanking Paine for the offer but
declining his services. Paine then asked Jefferson to persuade the
Virginia legislature to grant him land as a reward for his service
during the American Revolution. Jefferson wrote back there was
no hope of that happening.

Paine went to New York City from time to time. But he no
longer was a houseguest of the rich and famous. He met a man
named William Carver, who had been a child in Lewes when
Paine lived there. Carver had sometimes saddled Paine's horse
when he rode out on excise business. After coming to America,

he had done well as a blacksmith and veterinarian. Carver invited Paine to be his guest anytime he was in New York. Carver would consider it a great honor. At the end of July, Paine took him up on his offer. Paine was going up the stairs one evening when he had a sudden stroke and fell over the banister to the floor below. It did not affect his mind, but he was seriously injured in the fall. He could not get out of bed. A nurse had to be hired to wash and feed him for three months.

When he tried to leave Carver's house, he was presented with a bill for $150. Paine was shocked and refused to pay, saying he had been badly treated. He said that sometimes his only supper had been a slice of bread and butter. In answer, Carver wrote a lot of lies about Paine. He even went so far as to hint that Madame de Bonneville's sons were Paine's. Outraged at this falsehood, Madame de Bonneville immediately sued Carver for libel and she won the suit.

During the rest of his life, Paine avoided his farm and the isolation of New Rochelle. He lived in cheap boardinghouses in New York City or freeloaded with various people. He wrote all the time. His essay about yellow fever was widely read. Yellow fever caused many deaths in Savannah and New Orleans and other port cities like New York. Amazingly, Paine figured out that the cause of the sickness must come into the country in barrels and boxes from the West Indies and get into the air. This demonstrated how keen his mind was in making scientific deductions. Almost a hundred years later, it was discovered that yellow fever is spread by mosquitoes. They carry the virus and infect people with their bite. These mosquitoes can hide in barrels and boxes. Paine had suggested banning ships from the West Indies between June and October when the illness most often appeared in the United States. Thousands of lives might have been saved had Paine's advice been taken.

In 1807, Paine wrote several letters to Jefferson about the possibility of the United States' building a fleet of gunboats to protect its coasts. He carefully made a model of the boat he had in mind and sent it to Jefferson. The President kindly wrote back that he thought gunboats were a good idea. He sent the model and Paine's drawings to the Navy Department. The U.S. Navy was not interested.

Always in need of cash, in January 1808 Paine again wrote several letters to Congress. This time he asked to be reimbursed for his expenses on the 1781 trip to France with Colonel John Laurens. The next month he requested that Congress give him a reward for exposing Silas Deane, which had thereby saved the United States several million dollars. The requests were rejected for lack of supporting documents. No one in Congress personally remembered that Paine had done these things; all his old friends were retired or dead.

People who were hardly more than acquaintances finally had to take charge of his affairs. They made him sell his property in Bordentown. With that money, they paid someone to take care of him because his legs had become paralyzed. Paine, though bedridden, continued to write and to read the daily newspapers. When people came to visit him, he still greeted them by asking, "What news?" But none of his visitors were his famous friends from revolutionary days. In May 1809, he begged Madame de Bonneville to let him live at her house so he could spend his last days with friends. Madame de Bonneville took tender care of him. At the same time, she had to fend off clergymen coming to her house trying to get Paine to publicly take back the things he had written in *The Age of Reason*. He never did.

Paine died at eight o'clock in the morning, June 8, 1809. Madame de Bonneville buried him on his farm in New Rochelle. He had been denied burial in a Quaker cemetery. Although he was one of the most famous men of his time, very few people attended his funeral, certainly no "great men."

On his simple tombstone it read:

Thomas Paine
Author of common sense
Died June 8th, 1809
Aged 72 years

Despite his lifelong worries over money, in his will he left an

Thomas Paine's writings were praised and criticized by millions of American, French, and British readers.

estate of $10,000, a very good sum in 1809. Most of it went to Benjamin and Thomas Paine de Bonneville for their education.

As he had been a wanderer with no roots during life, a citizen of three countries, so he was destined to wander after death. In 1819, William Cobbett, the English journalist and writer who had once opposed Thomas Paine and the French Revolution but later became an admirer, traveled to New Rochelle. In the middle of the night he dug up Paine's bones and took them back to England.

But he did not bury them beside Paine's parents in Thetford. The bones were sold several times and eventually lost. Today, no one knows where Thomas Paine's remains are.

Yet Paine's ideas of liberty and equality for all live on. Although Paine did not invent these ideas, he was one of their greatest champions. He was able to explain them in language every man and woman could understand. These ideas have spread from country to country as people rise up and throw off their tyrannical rulers. Thomas Paine changed the world forever by helping to incite the American Revolution and by supporting the early stages of the French Revolution two hundred years ago. His weapon was not a gun. He used a more powerful one—his pen. He made people think. Because of Thomas Paine, the world was never the same.

1737	Thomas Pain is born on January 29 in Thetford, England.
1743-50	Pain attends school in Thetford.
1750	Pain leaves school to become an apprentice to his father, a stay maker.
1754	Pain runs away to sea.
1756	Pain spends a year on board a privateer.
1757	Pain works as a stay maker in London.
1759	Pain marries Mary Lambert.
1760	Mary Lambert dies.
1764	Pain is appointed excise tax collector in Alford.
1765	Pain is dismissed from the Excise Service.
1768	Pain is reappointed as excise tax collector.
1771	Pain marries Elizabeth Ollive.
1772-74	Pain works to secure a raise in pay for excise tax collectors.
1774	Pain is discharged from the Excise Service again. He is forced to sell possessions to pay creditors. Thomas and Elizabeth are legally separated. Pain sails for the American colonies and arrives in Philadelphia.
1775	Pain becomes editor of the *Pennsylvania Magazine*, but he is soon fired from his job.
1776	Pain publishes *Common Sense*. He changes the spelling of his name from Pain to Paine. Paine joins the fighting against the British during the American Revolution. He publishes *The American Crisis*.
1777	Paine is appointed secretary to the Committee for Foreign Affairs of the Congress.
1779	Resigned as secetary to the Committee for Foreign

Affairs and later in the year is appointed secretary to the Pennsylvania Assembly.

1781	Paine goes to France with Colonel John Laurens to secure money for the Continental Army.
1782	Paine signs a contract to write for Washington.
1783	Paine writes *Crisis Number XIII* as the Revolutionary War ends.
1784	The New York State Assembly awards Paine a farm in New Rochelle for his patriotic writing during the Revolutionary War.
1785	The Pennsylvania State Assembly awards Paine $2,250 for his writing during the war. Congress awards Paine $3,000 for services during the war.
1787	Paine arrives in France.
1791	Paine publishes *Part One* of *The Rights of Man*.
1792	Paine publishes *Part Two* of *The Rights of Man*. He is indicted by the British government for seditious libel. Paine flees from England to France where he takes a seat in the French National Convention as a delegate from Calais.
1793	Paine pleads to save the life of King Louis XVI of France. He is arrested and imprisoned in France.
1794	*Part One* of *The Age of Reason* is published. Paine is released from prison.
1795	*Part Two* of *The Age of Reason* is published.
1796	Paine's letter to George Washington is published.
1797	Napoleon consults with Paine.
1802	Paine returns to the United States.
1806	Paine suffers a stroke.
1809	Paine dies in New York City on June 8.

abdicate   To give up an official position of power, especially the position of king.

blasphemy   Great disrespect or contempt for God or for sacred persons or things.

catechism   A summary of religious doctrines and beliefs, often in the form of questions and answers.

counterrevolution   A revolution intended to undo an earlier revolution.

debtors' prison   A jail into which people who did not pay their debts were put. They stayed until their family or friends came up with the money to pay the debt.

effigy   An image or dummy of a hated person; the effigy was often hanged or burned in order to protest the hated person's activities.

flying camp   A group of troops formed for rapid movement from place to place.

guillotine   A machine designed to chop off people's heads by means of a heavy blade that slides down between vertical guides.

keelhaul   To punish a sailor by dragging the sailor under a ship in the water.

man-of-war   A warship.

manifesto A public proclamation or declaration of policy, purpose, or viewpoint.

meetinghouse A building used for public worship, especially for Quaker gatherings.

merchant ship A ship used in trade.

militia The body of citizens enrolled as a military force ready to serve in time of emergency.

natural history Science, the study of natural things.

open letter A published letter of protest or appeal usually addressed to a specific person but really intended for the general public.

orrery A piece of equipment showing the positions and motions of bodies in the solar system—the sun, the planets, and moons. These are represented by balls that move.

patent A government document giving the inventor rights to the invention for a limited number of years. A patent gives the inventor the right to prevent others from making, using, or selling the invention.

pen name An assumed name, used especially by authors of political books and pamphlets in the 18th century to avoid government prosecution.

pension A fixed sum paid regularly to a person, especially to a retired person or to his or her dependents.

press-gang A group of people with the power to force others into the armed forces, especially into the navy.

privateer   An armed private ship hired by a government to attack the merchant ships and warships of an enemy.

sans-culottes   Members of the revolutionary party at the time of the French Revolution who wanted a republic not a monarchy in France. These extreme radicals wore long pants rather than the short breeches worn by the upper classes.

seditious libel   Something written with the intention to encourage violent or illegal changes in the government or rebellion against the government.

stocks   A piece of equipment for publicly punishing people; it consisted of a wooden frame with holes in which the feet and hands could be locked.

Bordentown, New Jersey	• A commemorative plaque on the house Thomas Paine once owned
Morristown, New Jersey	• The Paine Statue
New Rochelle, New York	• Paine Monument, Paine cottage on his farm, Thomas Paine Historical Society Museum, grave site
Philadelphia, Pennsylvania	• Thomas Paine Collection at the American Philosophical Society, 105 South 5th Street, across from Independence Hall

BIBLIOGRAPHY

AND RECOMMENDED READINGS

Aldridge, Alfred Owen. *Man of Reason, The Life of Thomas Paine.* Philadelphia: Lippincott, 1959.

Ayer, A. J. *Thomas Paine.* New York: Atheneum, 1988.

Brodie, Fawn M. *Thomas Jefferson.* New York: Norton, 1974.

Burke, Edmund. *Reflections on the French Revolution.* Edited by Charles W. Eliot. The Harvard Classics. New York: Collier, 1963.

Common Sense, The Rights of Man, and Other Essential Writings of Thomas Paine. New York: New American Library, 1969.

The Complete Writings of Thomas Paine. Edited by Philip S. Foner. Vols. 1 and 2. New York: Citadel Press, 1969.

*Coolidge, Olivia. *Thomas Paine, Revolutionary.* New York: Scribner's, 1969.

Flexner, James Thomas. *George Washington in the American Revolution.* Boston: Little, Brown, 1967.

Foner, Eric. *Tom Paine and Revolutionary America.* New York: Oxford University Press, 1976.

*Gurko, Leo. *Tom Paine, Freedom's Apostle.* New York: Crowell,1957.

Hawke, David Freeman. *Paine.* New York: Harper and Row, 1974.

Life and Writings of Thomas Paine. Edited by Daniel Edwin Wheeler. Vols. 1, 2, and 3. New York: Vincent Parke, 1908.

McKay, John P., Bennett D. Hill, and John Buckler. *A History of Western Society.* Boston: Houghton, Mifflin, 1979.

*McKown, Robin. *Thomas Paine.* New York: Putnam's, 1962.

*Especially recommended for younger readers.

Smyth, Albert Henry. *The Writings of Benjamin Franklin.* Vol. 4. New York: Haskell House, 1907, 1970.

Sparks, Jared. *The Writings of George Washington.* Vols. 3, 4. Russell, Odiorne and Metcalf, 1834.

Van Doren, Carl. *Benjamin Franklin.* New York: Viking, 1938.

Williamson, Audrey. *Thomas Paine, His Life, Work and Times.* New York: St. Martin's Press, 1973.

Wright, Esmond. *Franklin of Philadelphia.* Cambridge: Belknap Press, Harvard University Press, 1986.

INDEX

Fr. = France; G.B. = Great Britain

Karin Clafford Farley is a lifelong resident of the Chicago area. She earned her bachelor's and master's degrees at the University of Illinois. Currently, she is a member of the faculty at the College of DuPage. Among previous books by the author is *Canal Boy*, a story about President James A. Garfield—20th President of the United States; *Harry S. Truman, The Man from Independence*; and *Robert H. Goddard*—a biography of the father of rocketry.

James P. Shenton is Professor of History at Columbia University. He has taught American History since 1951. Among his publications are *Robert John Walker, a Politician from Jackson to Lincoln*; *An Historian's History of the United States*; and *The Melting Pot*. Professor Shenton is a consultant to the National Endowment for the Humanities and has received the Mark Van Doren and Society of Columbia Graduates' Great Teachers Awards. He also serves as a consultant for CBS, NBC, and ABC educational programs.

COVER ILLUSTRATION

Gary McElhaney

MAPS

Go Media, Inc.

PHOTOGRAPHY CREDITS

P.6 The Bettmann Archive; p.10 North Wind Picture Archives; p.11 North Wind Picture Archives; p.13 The Bettmann Archive; p.14 North Wind Picture Archives; p.17 The Bettmann Archive; p.20 American Philosophical Society; p.22 Archives of St. Michael's-in-Lewes, England–© Edward Reeves; p.23 North Wind Picture Archives; p.25 North Wind Picture Archives; p.26 New York Public Library; p.28 Historical Pictures/Stock Montage; p.30 North Wind Picture Archives; p.33 North Wind Picture Archives; p.34 North Wind Picture Archives; p.39 The Bettmann Archive; p.41 North Wind Picture Archives; p.44 North Wind Picture Archives; p.45 North Wind Picture Archives; p.46 North Wind Picture Archives; p.48 Historical Pictures/Stock Montage; p.49 North Wind Picture Archives; p.51 North Wind Picture Archives; p.53 North Wind Picture Archives; p.55 North Wind Picture Archives; p.57 The Bettmann Archive; p.59 North Wind Picture Archives; p.64 North Wind Picture Archives; p.69 North Wind Picture Archives; p.70 Brown Brothers; p.74 The Bettmann Archive; p.77 The Bettmann Archive; p.79 American Philosophical Society; p.81 The Bettmann Archive; p.83 American Philosophical Society; p.85 Historical Pictures/Stock Montage; p.86 North Wind Picture Archives; p.89 The Bettmann Archive; p.91 Historical Pictures/Stock Montage; p.95 The Bettmann Archive; p.101 The Bettmann Archive; p.104 The Granger Collection; p.109 American Philosophical Society; p.112 The Bettmann Archive.